STOV

FRIENDS OF ACPL

S0-ERI-033

AUTHOR'S NOTE

We dedicate this book to all the young filmmakers who we hope will find meaningful ways of communicating the ideas of understanding and peace.

Jeanne and Bob Bendick

Copyright © 1970 by Jeanne and Robert Bendick

All Rights Reserved.
Printed in the United States of America.

No part of this publication may be reproduced,
stored in a retrieval system, or transmitted,
in any form or by any means, electronic, mechanical,
photocopying, recording, or otherwise, without the
prior written permission of the publisher.

Library of Congress Catalog Card Number: 79-127965

1234567890 HDBP 7654321070

	PAGE
Welcome to the World of the Movie Makers	4
Who Makes a Film?	8
Outlines and Scripts	12
Budgets	18
Your Production Schedule	26
Filming	30
What Is a Moving Picture?	40
What Size Are You Going to Work in?	41
Cameras	42
Choosing a Camera What Kind?	43
Lenses	48
Filming Accessories	52
Film	54
Lighting	57
Sound	60
A Bag of Tricks	64
Titles and Credits	66
Animation	67
Processing	70
Editing	72
Projectors	79
Projection Screens	83
Where Your Film Can Be Shown	84
Filming Words	85
Some Handy Charts	
Which Lens for Which Picture?	91
Camera Shutter Speed Table	91
Running Times and Film Lengths	92
Sources and Periodicals	93
Index	95

WELCOME TO THE WORLD OF THE MOVIE MAKERS

Welcome to a creative world filled with excitement, imagination, experimentation, beauty, despair, fun, and satisfaction.

Welcome to a world where, with the simplest of equipment, you can create a film that will make people laugh, or cry, think, learn or wonder; where you can communicate what you feel, see, want, remember, know, to the whole world or just to yourself.

Welcome to a world in which you can be a lone creator or one of a team.

The film world once belonged only to the professionals. Movie making was complicated and expensive. Some movies still are. But now, equipment has been vastly simplified. The technical results can almost be guaranteed; costs can be fitted to the purse.

Movies have shifted from being mostly an entertainment medium to a powerful way in which people communicate with each other, even if they don't speak the same language.

If you feel something or want to say something, you can say it with a film.

That's what this book is all about. It's a basic exploration of how movie making works—how you make a film.

You can use more or less of this information as you move along in your film making. Use it as a guide, but don't let it stifle your imagination or limit your experimentation. Good film making is creative.

Before you make a film, decide:
what you want to say,
who you want to say it to,
and how you want to say it.

As your film takes shape you will probably find it changing. Don't be afraid to let it change. Part of being a filmmaker is letting your ideas change as your film grows.

Your film could be a comedy, a tragedy, history, or mystery, generally in the form of a story.

Your film could be a documentary. A documentary selects a particular subject from life and tells about it as it is.

Your film might show how to do something—make a birdhouse, fix a motor, play basketball, sell magazines.

You might want to report an event with film. A football game is an event. So is a fire. So is a wedding, or the opening of a butterfly.

Sometimes people make films to express a mood or a feeling. The film may be just impressions. The filmmaker may see one thing in it, and each person in the audience may see something different. It depends on what each one brings to the film.

The best way to learn about films is by filming. But you can learn a lot about movie making by looking at movies too. When you see a film that you like, try to decide what is good or bad about it. How has the filmmaker communicated his ideas and feelings?

Is it the story?
Is it the photography?
Is it the direction?
Is it the editing?

Probably it is a combination of all these things. You can't really study a film by seeing it through once. See it several times, at one sitting if you have to. After the first time you will be able to concentrate on the techniques in the film, not just on the story. You will get to know how other filmmakers work. And you will understand how—and why— each one photographs and puts a film together in a certain way. A good filmmaker has a style of his own, just as a good painter or a good writer does.

IN 1872, AN ENGLISH PHOTOGRAPHER NAMED EADWEARD MUYBRIDGE MADE THE FIRST SUCCESSFUL PICTURES OF A MOTION. USING 24 STILL CAMERAS, HE PHOTOGRAPHED A RUNNING HORSE. AS THE HORSE PASSED EACH CAMERA, HE BROKE A STRING WHICH TRIPPED THE SHUTTER.

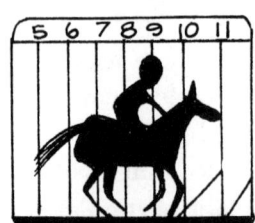

WHEN THE PICTURES WERE PROJECTED IN QUICK SUCCESSION, THEY GAVE A PICTURE OF MOTION.

Keep in touch with what other young filmmakers are doing. You can do this through:

> The Young Filmmakers Foundation
> 310 West 53 Street
> New York, N.Y. 10019

A number of groups have film festivals which show the work of young filmmakers. For information about these, write to:

> The American Film Institute
> Education Division
> 1815 H Street N.W.
> Washington, D.C. 20006

This is a private, non-profit agency interested in all film making.

> CINE
> 16th Street N.W.
> Washington, D.C. 20036

This is a government agency that chooses films to enter in film festivals around the world. It has an amateur section.

> International Centre of Films for Children and Young People
> Secretariat General
> 141 rue Royale
> Brussels, 3 Belgium

This agency arranges festivals all over the world for movies made by young filmmakers.

Read articles about film making and filmmakers in newspapers and magazines. The names of some you can subscribe to are listed in the back of the book.

EDISON BUILT THE FIRST MOVIE STUDIO IN 1893.

THE "BLACK MARIA" WAS MADE OF TARPAPER. IT WAS ON A PLATFORM THAT COULD BE TURNED TO LET SUN IN.

WHO MAKES A FILM?

It takes many skills to produce a film. Depending on the size of the production, one person or a dozen or a hundred people may bring those skills to it. But certain basic jobs have to be done in every film, whether they are done by one person or many.

The person who does each job has a title.
THE PRODUCER supervises the whole film. He gets the idea; raises the money; chooses the other people he needs to work on or act in the film. He arranges ways and places for showing the film.
THE DIRECTOR has the overall creative view of the film, and he directs every element in the film toward that concept. He figures out how the idea is to be translated into visual form. He chooses the locations. He works with the art director, the set designer, and the costumer. He decides where, and how, the camera is to be used. He directs the actors if there are any. He supervises the editing so the scenes are put together in the best way to tell the story as he wants it.
THE WRITER writes the original script or outline, or adapts an existing story for a film. Or he writes a narration for the film after it has been edited.
THE CAMERAMAN uses his technical knowledge to get the pictures the director wants. He supervises the lighting. (In a large production, the head cameraman, or *cinematographer,* sets up the composition and movement of the camera but does not run the camera. The operating cameraman runs the camera, and *his* assistant controls any lens changes or focus changes.)

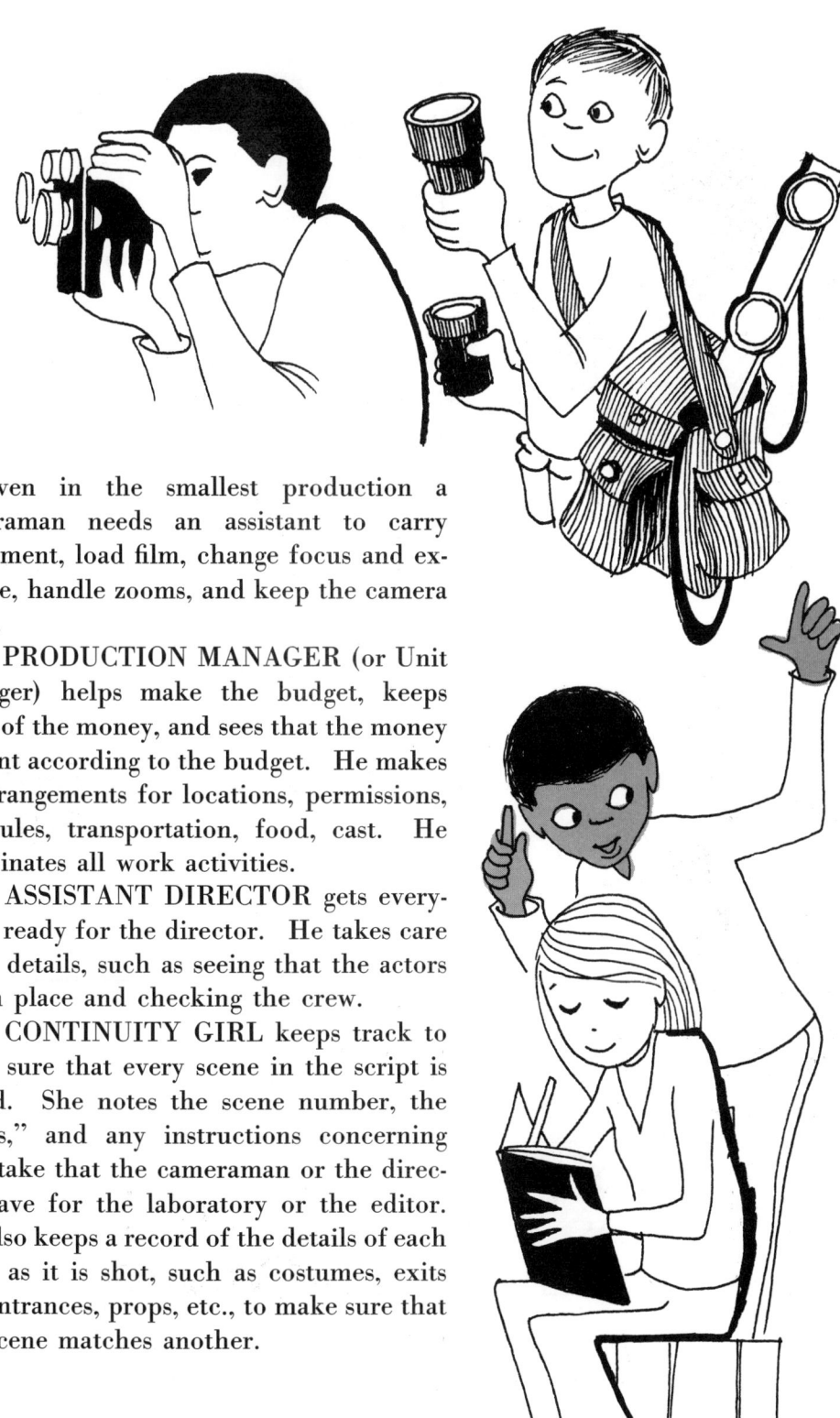

Even in the smallest production a cameraman needs an assistant to carry equipment, load film, change focus and exposure, handle zooms, and keep the camera clean.

THE PRODUCTION MANAGER (or Unit Manager) helps make the budget, keeps track of the money, and sees that the money is spent according to the budget. He makes all arrangements for locations, permissions, schedules, transportation, food, cast. He coordinates all work activities.

THE ASSISTANT DIRECTOR gets everything ready for the director. He takes care of all details, such as seeing that the actors are in place and checking the crew.

THE CONTINUITY GIRL keeps track to make sure that every scene in the script is filmed. She notes the scene number, the "takes," and any instructions concerning each take that the cameraman or the director have for the laboratory or the editor. She also keeps a record of the details of each scene as it is shot, such as costumes, exits and entrances, props, etc., to make sure that one scene matches another.

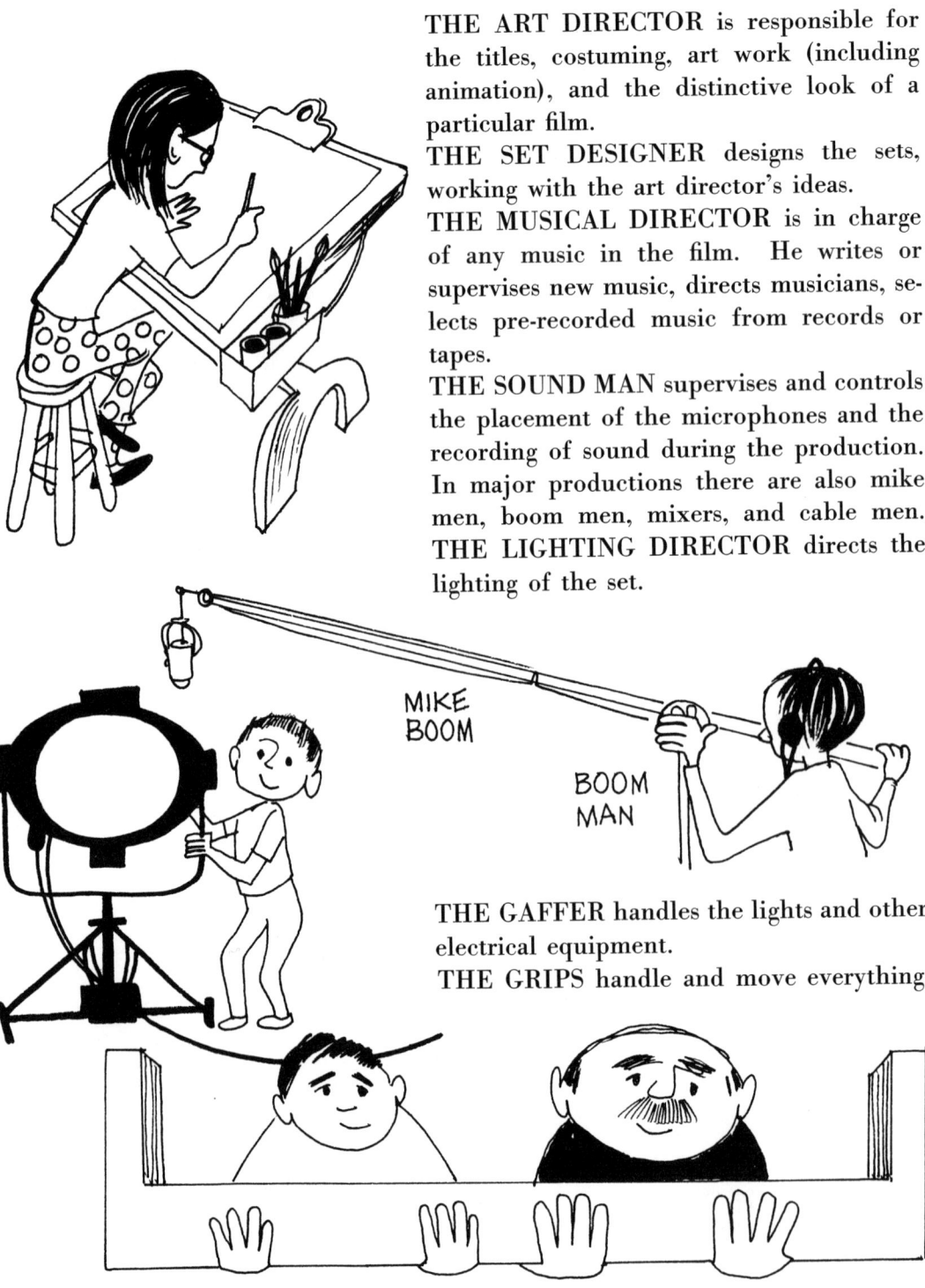

THE ART DIRECTOR is responsible for the titles, costuming, art work (including animation), and the distinctive look of a particular film.

THE SET DESIGNER designs the sets, working with the art director's ideas.

THE MUSICAL DIRECTOR is in charge of any music in the film. He writes or supervises new music, directs musicians, selects pre-recorded music from records or tapes.

THE SOUND MAN supervises and controls the placement of the microphones and the recording of sound during the production. In major productions there are also mike men, boom men, mixers, and cable men.

THE LIGHTING DIRECTOR directs the lighting of the set.

MIKE BOOM

BOOM MAN

THE GAFFER handles the lights and other electrical equipment.

THE GRIPS handle and move everything.

THE PROP MAN gets and is responsible for the props (or properties). A prop is some object that is to be used in the film, such as a pistol, a pair of glasses, an Eskimo hunting spear, or a roast chicken.

THE EDITOR, working with the script or outline, selects the shots and scenes and puts them together in the order which he thinks tells the story best. Either the editor or his assistant splices the film together.

In commercial filming there are strict regulations about who does what job. If your production staff is limited, you can combine jobs and responsibilities, for example:

    Producer–Writer
    Director–Cameraman–Editor
    Production Manager–Assistant Director
    Art Director–Set Designer–Prop Man
    Assistant Cameraman–Sound Man–Grip

In a small crew everybody lends a hand to do what needs doing. You can make any job combinations you want, depending on the number of people you have and what they can do. But *all* these jobs must be done if the production—whatever size—is to be made effectively and economically.

You can make a film by yourself. You may not think that your film has an art director, but when you decide what color titles to make, you are an art director. When you decide what kind of chair an actor sits in, you are a set designer. When you tell the actors where to stand, you're a director. And when you start worrying about money, you're a producer.

OUTLINES AND SCRIPTS

The best way to begin to work on a film is to write out a description of the film you want to make. You may change some of your thinking as your filming goes along, but writing out your ideas will give you a good way to start thinking about what you want to do.

The description should include what you want to communicate; your viewpoint about it; and what audience you are making the film for. When you know what you want your film to do, you can translate your idea into a more detailed outline or script.

Different kinds of films require different kinds of preparations and different kinds of scripts.

REPORTING EVENTS

When you report an event on film, you show all the important things about it so that when the film is edited an audience gets an impression of exactly what happened. Because reporting means telling the facts as they took place, a prepared script is impossible. What you do need is all the information about where the event is going to take place; when; a description and schedule of the parts of the event; who the important people are.

The assignment sheet for reporting an event might look like this:

Event: Campaign for Mayor. Opening speech by challenging candidate.
Date: September 12th
Place: City Hall Park
Schedule: 11:45 A.M.   Short concert by local jazz combo.
              12:00 noon   Candidate arrives, accompanied by Congressman Jones who will introduce him.
              12:05 P.M.   Photographs. Introduction by Jones.
              12:10 P.M.   Candidate speaks. (Copies of speech will be available at 11:30 from Press Aide.) Speech approximately 20 minutes.
Get general coverage with plenty of reaction. Look for signs.
Contacts: Press Aide, Mr. B. Brown, Police Sergeant Gibson

DOCUMENTARY FILMS

Before you make a documentary, you have to do a lot of research so that you really understand the subject of your film. This means seeing the subject first hand, reading about it, talking to people who are part of it. When you feel that you really know your subject, write down all your ideas about what you want to say and what your approach is going to be.

Then, working from those notes, make an outline, listing the types of scenes and the people and the places that will illustrate best what you are trying to show. You can't be (and don't want to be) too precise in describing your scenes because when you are actually filming you will want to take advantage of the best things that happen in front of your camera.

Part of your outline might look like this:

Title: Portrait of a Candidate.
Objective: To show what the challenging candidate for mayor is like and how the campaign changes him, if it does.
1. *Early History.*
    Get family pictures, school yearbook, home movies.
2. *Present Personal Life.*
    Film: Candidate at home
        Family
        Hobbies
        Sports
        As Scout Leader
3. *Present Professional Life.*
    Film: At his law office
        In court
        Conducting school board meeting
4. *Political Activities Connected with Campaign.*
    Film: Planning strategy meeting with aides
        Addressing business group to raise funds
        Speeches and rallies around town
        ... (and much more)
This is only a partial list of what you would film.

Before you shoot each segment, make notes of what you want to get out of it. Don't get sidetracked and forget the objective of your film. Because your documentary is to show the portrait of a man running for office and what he has to go through as a candidate, you are more interested in him and how he acts than in the issues of the campaign. (The issues would be a different documentary.)

To show the man in action, you would cover a number of speeches and rallies, concentrating on a different thing each time. Part of the outline shot list for the speech in City Hall Park might look like this:

Shot list.
1. Wide, establishing shot of City Hall Park just before the candidate arrives.
2. Series of close-ups of people waiting to show kinds of people and attitude.
3. Signs and posters in crowd.
4. Walking, over-the-shoulder shot of candidate as he moves toward platform through police and crowd.
5. If possible, second camera moving through same crowd, giving candidate's point of view. (Short lens, close-ups of people.)
6. Reverse close-up of candidate from #4 as he mounts platform and looks out at crowd.

... (and more.)

NOTES: During speech and directly after, concentrate on close-ups and extreme close-ups of candidate to show intensity and strain.
Get plenty of close-up reaction, one and two shots; also hands applauding; also hostile or no reaction shots. Close, over-the-shoulder, walking shot as candidate leaves, possibly to compare with entering shot.

SOUND: Record speech and all background sound.

A WALKING, OVER-THE-SHOULDER SHOT

Keep notes on every scene you film so that you cover everything on the shot list. Also keep a record of the scenes that "just happen" while you are filming.

Once you start editing, you will combine your original outline, your actual shot list, and what "feels" right to put the film together.

The final narration for a documentary is written from the edited film and combined with the sound that you record on location.

Sometimes filmmakers make documentaries without any written outline at all. But when they do, the outline is there anyway, in their heads. Some documentaries are very personal things and just grow out of the way a filmmaker reacts to what he sees as he is filming.

No film can show everything about any real life situation, so your selection of what you are going to show establishes what the audience is going to get from your film. You may be all for something or all against it. Or you may balance the facts so the audience gets a rounded picture. A documentary that is all for, or against, something is more of a propaganda film than a documentary.

DRAMATIC STORIES

A story-telling or dramatic script is the most detailed right from the beginning, even if it has no dialog. You can write in the details right away because you are making it all up. First the plot of the story is outlined. Then that is expanded to show the way in which the characters act out the plot. This outline is expanded again, by listing each shot of the action. The script for a dramatic film also includes descriptions of locations, scenery, costumes, actors' movements, lighting effects, and often camera movements and angles.

"THE GREAT TRAIN ROBBERY," (1903) WAS ONE OF THE FIRST DRAMATIC FILMS.

EDWIN S. PORTER WAS THE DIRECTOR

If the script is for a sound film, all dialog and sound effects are included too.

Every shot in every scene is numbered. The beginning of one sequence of a dramatic shooting script might look like this:

Location: A small park across the street from City Hall. The City Hall is a three-story, gray, stone building, built about 1920. Stone steps lead from the main door down to the street. To the right is the courtroom entrance.

The park has a few tired trees. At one end there is a statue of a World War I soldier. A wooden platform has been erected at the end of the park nearest City Hall. Bunting is draped on the front.

About 100 people are gathered around the platform, more men than women. Most of them are workers on their lunch hour. A few munch sandwiches or candy bars.

A four man jazz combo in striped shirts sit to the left of the stand. They have just finished playing.

	CAMERA	SOUND
Scene 121	MCU of technician fooling with microphone on platform. Technician hears something out of frame, looks toward City Hall, makes final adjustment, and moves to rear of platform and down stairs. Camera follows and picks up candidate and aides, who have just come through courtroom door. Zoom in to candidate.	Technician: Testing 1 2 3 4, 1 2 3 4. (Hear sound through park PA system.) General background sound. Combo strikes up a few bars.

	CAMERA	SOUND
Scene 122	Two shot of candidate and aide hurrying toward platform. Candidate looks upset.	Candidate: "Gee, not much of a crowd! Did you put the posters up last night?" Aide: "We got them up okay, but when we checked this morning, half of them had been torn down. And where's Jones? He's supposed to introduce you!"
Scene 123	CU of aide. Nods head, but looks worried.	

The above represents only a minute or so of screen time. Depending on the length and complexity of the film, the shooting script for a dramatic movie can be as thick as a big city phone book.

Not all dramatic movies use such controlled scripts. Many dramatic scenes are played in real locations where things are happening that influence the actors and the action in a way that is not part of the script. This free blending of dramatic action and reality makes a film more vital.

Imagination is an important part of all film making. Don't feel that just because something is written down you have to stick to it. The purpose of a script is to keep your imagination organized.

All budgets, production plans, casting and hiring, schedules, and editing begin with and are guided by the outline or script.

BUDGETS

A budget is what you decide you are going to spend on a film. Everything in a professional film costs money. Here are some of the major items in a professional film budget:
1. Producer's, director's, writer's salaries.
2. Cast salaries.
3. Crew salaries.
4. Purchase or rental of equipment (cameras, camera accessories, lights, sound equipment, editing equipment).
5. Rental of studio.
6. Location fees.
7. Rights fees.
8. Food and transportation.
9. Costumes.
10. Scenery and props.
11. Raw stock (film).
12. Developing costs.
13. Work print.
14. Optical effects.
15. Answer prints.
16. Release prints.
17. Film editor and assistants.
18. Rental of editing room.
19. Editing supplies.
20. Sound tape.
21. Titles.
22. Animation.
23. Overhead (telephone, insurance, legal fees, secretaries' salaries, office rent, accounting, taxes).

In your budget, you have to provide for all the same things. But there are many things you can do without cash.

Expenses	Notes and Substitutes	Cash Outlay
1. Producer's, director's, writer's salaries	You and your friends. But you must make an honest appraisal of talents (and willingness to work) before assigning jobs. You need *talent*, even if it's free.	None
2. Cast salaries	Everybody likes to act. A cast party can be the pay.	None
3. Crew salaries	You and friends. But item 1 applies here too.	None
4. Purchase or rental of equipment	While it might be possible to borrow a camera, a tape recorder, editing equipment, and a projector, people don't like to lend them. It is better to buy equipment you will be using all the time. Rent items you will use only occasionally.	Super 8 mm cameras start at about $30. new. Viewers for editing start at about $20. Projectors start at about $50. Splicer, $5.00 Prices and rental fees are in catalogs that you can send for. (See p. 93)
5. Rental of studio	You could use a gym, hall, store, but you may have to pay a custodian to keep it open. You might be able to borrow a room in someone's house.	Possible custodian fee.

Expenses	Notes and Substitutes	Cash Outlay
6. Location fees	Care in using the property and cleaning it up when you are finished. Schedule your filming when it does not interfere with the normal activities at the location.	None
7. Rights fees	If you are using a published story, play, or music, be sure to check with the publisher. There are special royalties for students, but you will probably have to pay something if you are going to charge admission to your film.	Possible royalty.
8. Food and transportation	If you are taking people on location, you should supply a way to get there and food while they are working. Friends and relatives might supply both. Otherwise allow for this in the budget. Remember that filming is hard work and people get tired, hungry, crabby, and non-productive. A small treat keeps the morale up.	Possible carfare, sandwich, coke or candy money.
9. Costumes	If you need them, in most cases, costumes can be borrowed or improvised. Historical costumes may have to be rented, but rentals are expensive. If you are going to make costumes, you will have to pay for the material. Enlist talented friends and relatives for sewing.	Possible rental expenses, cost of material, sewing supplies, cleaning if clothes are borrowed.

Expenses	Notes and Substitutes	Cash Outlay
10. Scenery and props	Scenery is expensive to make or rent. If possible, use existing locations and borrow props. Imaginative use of a few objects can suggest an elaborate background.	Expensive if you are going to build or rent. None if you substitute imagination.
11. Raw stock (film)	This costs money. You have to have it, and there's almost no way of getting it free. Super 8 mm color and black and white cost the same. 16 mm black and white film costs about half of what color does, so in the beginning stages of your movie making, use it, if you are working in 16 mm. Many fine films are made in black and white. The more film you use, the more money you spend. The more carefully you plan your film, the less film you will need. If you *really* have almost no money at all, sometimes you can get outdated film from supply houses for very little money, or even free. But test it first.	8 mm, double 25′ B&W $ 2.50 Color $ 2.50 Super 8 mm Cartridge, 50′ B&W $ 2.65 Color $ 2.60 16 mm, 100′ daylight load B&W $ 5.50 Color $ 8.00
12. Developing	The developing cost may be included in the price of the raw stock. If it is not, the price is approximately . . .	Super 8 mm, 50′ cartridge B&W $ 2.85 Color $ 2.25 16 mm B&W reversal 100′ roll $ 3.25 B&W negative 100′ roll $ 3.25 Color 100′ roll $ 5.45

Expenses	Notes and Substitutes	Cash Outlay
13. Work print	If you plan to edit and project the original developed film, you do not need a work print. If you do plan on using a work print, you can save money if you make a black and white work print for editing, even if your film is in color.	Super 8 mm Color $.11 a foot B&W $.09 a foot 16 mm Color $.10 a foot B&W from negative, $.08 a foot from reversal $.08 a foot
14. Optical effects	Optical work is expensive. Wherever possible, do it in the camera. A 16 mm fade done in the lab costs about ... A dissolve done in the lab costs about ...	$ 3.00, color $ 6.50, color
15. Answer print	Not needed if you plan to edit and project the original footage. If you make an answer print, these will be approximate costs	Super 8 mm Color, $.135 a foot B&W, $.095 a foot 16 mm Color, $.14 a foot B&W, $.06 a foot
16. Release print	Not needed if you plan to project your original, edited material. If you make release prints, they cost about ...	16 mm Color $.11 a foot
17. Film editor and assistants	This is a critical job. Do it yourself.	None
18. Rental of editing room	This might be a room in your house. But it must be a place where the film you are editing can be left untouched while you are working on it.	None, if you have cooperation.

Expenses	Notes and Substitutes	Cash Outlay
19. Editing supplies 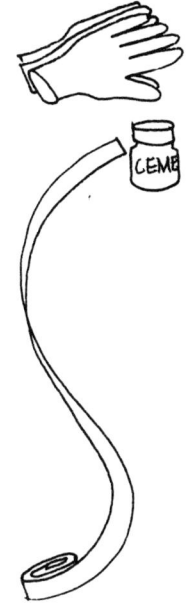	You need cement, splicing tape, leader material, marking pencils, gloves, reels, rewinds. (See *Editing* for other editing equipment)	Cement $.50 for a 1 oz. bottle. Splicing tape: double perforated, 16 mm roll $ 6.00 non-perforated, $ 1.50 8 mm roll, $ 1.60 Reels: 16 mm, 400' $ .60 800' $ 1.50 8 mm 400' $ .32 Leader: 16 mm 1000' $10.00 8 mm 1000' $15.00 Gloves, 1 doz $ 2.70 Marking pencils, 1 doz $ 3.00
20. Sound tape 	¼-inch tape costs money, but by shopping around and testing bargains for brittleness and fidelity you can save money. And remember, you can reuse tape.	New, 600' roll $1.50
21. Titles and credits 	Can be very expensive. But with lots of imagination you can do your own for just film cost. Screen credits can be a form of advertising and a valuable exchange for goods and services you may not be able to afford to pay cash for.	Cost of film used.

Expenses	Notes and Substitutes	Cash Outlay
22. Animation	Because it takes a lot of time, professional animation is very expensive. But if you and your friends are working free, you can make excellent and imaginative animations for very little money.	Film cost plus art supplies.
23. Overhead:	About 10 or fifteen per cent of the cost of a professional production is overhead.	
Telephone	There are always a lot of telephone calls connected with making a film. Somebody has to pay for them.	Phone calls
Insurance	It is a good idea to insure equipment against loss or damage and people against accidents. Schools and community centers usually have ways of getting insurance at low rates.	Insurance
Legal fees, office help, rent, taxes, accounting	Some legal work and accounting might have to be done in connection with your production. Enlist legal or accounting friends or relatives, and be appreciative.	None

Your budget is the amount that you plan (and hope) the picture will cost. Unless you keep track of *all* expenses as you go along, you won't know if you are keeping within your budget. And you won't be able to make corrections, or save on other items, in time.

SOME SUGGESTIONS FOR FINANCING YOUR FILM

1. In a school, sponsorship by the PTA or a similar parents' organization.
2. If you belong to a school film group or neighborhood film club, solicit the sponsorship of local merchants. It's good public relations for them. Acknowledge their help in your screen credits.
3. If the subject matter is some neighborhood problem or project, you might get donations of film, processing, and equipment from local camera stores or laboratories.
4. If your film group is in a neighborhood community center, your city may have money for supporting such projects. Be sure to find out about this in your community.
5. For *serious*, talented young filmmakers, there are some foundations that underwrite worthwhile film projects. For more information about these, write to the

    American Film Institute
    1815 H Street N.W.
    Washington, D.C. 20006

6. Check various film-making magazines in your local library for other sources of financial help.

One of the hardest and most important parts of a producer's job, amateur or professional, is raising money to finance his picture. Even if you charge admission for viewing the film at a neighborhood center or in the school auditorium, any money you make comes after the picture is finished. It can only be used for repaying.

SOME MONEY-RAISING IDEAS

YOUR PRODUCTION SCHEDULE

In a professional film production things are done in a certain order. Even if your production is very simple, all these things must be done.

1. Make out a schedule.

Proper scheduling is the key to efficient production. You schedule to make things happen in the right place at the right time. This means that some things will have to be done ahead of others so that everything is ready when you need it during the production. Not every thing (or every person) is needed right from the beginning or every day.

Decide on a starting day, and lay out a shooting schedule. Scenes are not usually shot in the order in which they will appear in the finished film. Generally, all the scenes in one location, or on one set, are filmed before starting at another location. Keep this in mind when you make your schedule.

If some of your shooting is outdoors and some indoors, schedule the outdoor scenes first, but have everything standing by to do indoor scenes instead if the weather is bad. In this way you make the best use of your crew and time.

Before scheduling your crew members, be sure they will be available when you need them. Professional crews are sometimes busy on other jobs. Amateur crews sometimes have other jobs or commitments too.

EVERYTHING SHOULD BE PLANNED BACK FROM THE DAY YOU WANT TO FINISH

TRY TO KEEP YOUR SHOOTING SCHEDULE ELASTIC

2. When you have made out your schedule, decide, from your outline or script, when you need cast, production crew, editors.

Editing should start when the first film comes back from processing. The editor is responsible for the care, condition, and storage of all film from this point on. He should store the original, if there is one, and work with the work print.

If the developed film is on a core, it should be put on a reel, with head and tail leaders.

Film should be screened and scenes listed.

A rough cut of each sequence should be assembled.

16mm FILM OFTEN COMES BACK FROM PROCESSING ON A CORE, WITH NO REEL

MOUNT THE FILM. PUT LEADER AT THE HEAD AND TAIL

3. Make arrangements for your basic studio space. When you are looking for an indoor place to film, look for these things:

Is there electric power and outlets? Can you hang lights?

Will you have to mix daylight and artificial light? (This creates color problems.)

Is there a place to build scenery? A way to bring it into the studio? Somewhere to move it out of the way?

Is the floor smooth if you are going to dolly the camera?

Can you get permission to film in the building?

If you are going to shoot sound, you need a sound studio. Otherwise outside noises will keep spoiling your sound track.

4. Locations should be scouted long before production starts so you can make necessary arrangements or resolve any special problems connected with them.

In many towns and cities the police department or other city bureaus issue permits to film on the streets, in the parks, or in public buildings. Be sure to arrange for these ahead of time.

Arrange transportation to locations.

5. Get together all your equipment and check it over carefully. Reserve any equipment you need to rent.

6. Figure out how much film you will need, and order it well in advance so you can get the same emulsion number for your entire production. This will give you much better color matching.

7. Make arrangements with a laboratory to develop your film as quickly as possible. Set up a standard arrangement for getting the film to them and getting it back, either by messenger or express.

8. Have a place set up to screen the "rushes," or "dailies." The director, the cameraman, the editor, and the cast should be there to see them.

9. If you have a definite deadline for showing your film, make sure that you figure the time needed after your film is edited, for titles, optical work, and prints.

A schedule chart is a good way to make sure that everyone knows what is needed and what has to be done by any date during the production. It is also a good way to check that things *have* been done.

No two production charts are ever alike. Make yours to fit your production. Part of it might look like this:

SHOOTING SCHEDULE
JOE FOR MAYOR

JULY	1	2	3	4	5	6	7	8	9	10
SHOOTING SCRIPT COMPLETED	✓									
SURVEYS		BUS STOP	DINER	PARK	COURT ROOM					
PROPS READY						BUS BENCH	PARK STAND			
RENTAL EQUIPMENT DEL						DOLLY	DOLLY LIGHTS	DOLLY	DOLLY	DOLLY LIGHTS
CAST REHEARSAL			✓	✓	✓					
SHOOTING - LOCATION				BUS STOP	BUS STOP	BUS STOP	DINER	PARK	PARK	DINER
SHOOTING - CAST						✓	✓	✓	✓	✓
CAMERAMAN				✓	✓	✓	✓	✓	✓	✓
DIRECTOR			✓	✓	✓	✓	✓	✓	✓	✓
PRODUCTION MANAGER		✓	✓	✓	✓	✓	✓	✓	✓	✓
EDITING STARTS								✓	✓	✓
FINISH EDITING										
SHOOT TITLES										
OPTICALS										

FILMING
BASICS

The best way to learn about filming is to make films. But no matter how clearly you know what you want to do, you can't put anything in your finished film that doesn't come through your camera. Know your camera and the film you are using before you start. Having to learn about them in the middle of a production is frustrating and expensive.

You can't make a movie unless you get the image you want on the film. That means that the exposure should be correct for the effect you want to get, and the things you want in focus should be in focus.

Exposure

When raw film is exposed to light coming through the lens of your camera a latent image forms on the film. If there is too much light, the film is overexposed. Everything looks very pale when the picture is developed. When not enough light falls on the film, the film is underexposed. Then the picture looks very dark.

Exposure depends on four factors:
1. The amount of light on the scene.
2. The speed of your film.
3. The shutter speed of your camera.
4. The size opening of your lens.

If you don't have a light meter, use the exposure guide that comes in the film box. If the camera has a built-in light meter, it will automatically set your camera to the correct exposure or indicate the f stop for you to set the camera lens at.

30

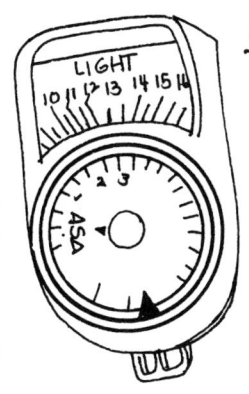

A METER THAT READS REFLECTED LIGHT IS A GOOD GENERAL METER

There are two kinds of separate light meters. One measures the light that is reflected from an object. The other kind measures the light that is falling on the object. The reflective meter is less expensive and more generally used.

Set the meter to the speed rating of the film you are using. The rating is generally different for artificial and outdoor light. A light meter reads the amount of light on the subject and tells you what f stop to use at any particular shutter speed. (Be sure to get the instruction book for your particular meter, even if you get the meter second hand.)

Focus

Objects that are in focus are sharp in the picture. If you have a fixed focus lens, only objects at a particular distance are *really* sharp. Everything else is acceptably, but not sharply, in focus.

If you have a focusing lens, you can set the lens to the distance that will put what you want in focus. If your camera allows you to look through the lens, you can see what's in focus as you focus the lens.

The smaller the opening in the lens (the larger the f stop number), the more things will be in focus from near to far. Another way of saying this is, the greater your depth of focus will be.

 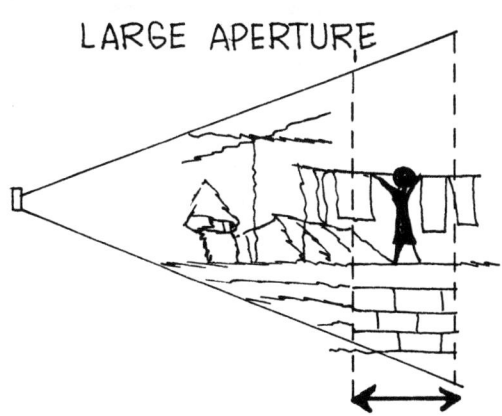

EVERYTHING BETWEEN THE ARROWS WOULD BE IN FOCUS

31

DON'T SHOOT THROUGH A CLOSED WINDOW. YOU WILL GET REFLECTIONS

Another way of filming a street scene is to conceal the camera and follow the action with a long lens. A car, a small truck, or a second floor window are good hiding places. If the actors are going to move any distance, the camera should be high enough to keep them in view.

Sometimes the camera is concealed in a suitcase, a lunch box, or a guitar. If you film this way, use a wide-angle lens and stay close to the actors. You can only point the camera and hope that you are framing the action. Ingenuity is the key to working under these conditions.

It is much easier to film this way if you are not using sync sound. If you are, you have to use wireless microphones and that gets complicated. If you want background or "wild" sound, retrace the route of the action right after the filming and record the sound.

The documentary, or cinéma vérité, style is another way of filming. This means filming, as realistically as possible, exactly what is happening in a real life situation. You select the time, place, and event that you want to film. But you do not interfere in any way or try to control what happens, not even with a "Look to your left" or "Okay, we're set."

The key idea in this kind of shooting is to be unobtrusive. Use the least possible crew. If the shooting is silent, only the cameraman should be in the middle of things. If light has to be used and the action is moving, the assistant cameraman or the director can carry a couple of sun guns, the extra film, and anything else that is needed.

When you are filming people in a real situation do not talk to them while you are filming. Do not get involved. If possible, they should not think of you any more than they would a tree or a piece of furniture.

In documentary filming or news reporting be sure to cover the subject thoroughly. That's what "documenting" and "reporting" mean. It is easy to misrepresent any situation with film. By filming only what you want to show and leaving out the scenes that give a different point of view, it is easy to corrupt the truth.

As a filmmaker you have a great responsibility in the way you use this power. It can be effective and dramatic in a story-telling film. But it can be destructive as well as dishonest when you are supposedly telling the facts.

In communicating ideas, pictorial symbols can be a kind of shorthand for a feeling or a whole action. A rat can symbolize dirt and poverty; an empty bowl, hunger; one face, the condition of a whole group of people. Some single shots can suggest a whole series of events—a toy in the rubble; a heel grinding eyeglasses into the pavement; fireworks.

SUGGESTIONS THAT CAN MAKE FILMING EASIER

Probably a good deal of your filming will be with a hand-held camera. It is almost essential that you have a reflex finder for this kind of work. You could not keep your picture in focus or frame with an auxiliary finder.

Learn and practice how to move with the camera. Learn to walk with it while you're filming and to move the camera in any direction as you follow the action. Learn how to work with a zoom lens, change focus, and change exposure all while you're moving. Reality in filming is no excuse for rocky, out-of-focus picture taking.

There are times when a move is too complex for a cameraman alone. He needs someone to help him handle some of the camera adjustments. In some moves, backward or forward, it's a big help to have someone steer, like this:

Where the cameraman himself has to make focus, zoom, and exposure changes, he is sometimes handicapped by not being able to adjust quickly to changing action. Many times the film which is exposed while he is making these changes is not usable. So he must be sure to film an insert scene afterwards that can be cut in as a bridge.

IT'S A BIG HELP TO HAVE AN ASSISTANT WHO WILL KEEP PASSERS-BY FROM WALKING IN FRONT OF THE CAMERA

Lighting conditions may vary a great deal in a long, continuing shot. If it is possible, first walk through the entire sequence with your exposure meter, taking readings as you go. Then you'll have to remember where to make your f stop changes when you are filming.

If it is not possible to do this, take a number of readings in bright and shadowy places right around you to get the range of lighting conditions you will meet when you make your actual move. Or you may have a helper with an exposure meter moving with you, taking readings and making the f stop changes. With practice, after taking an initial reading, you will be able to estimate light changes without the meter.

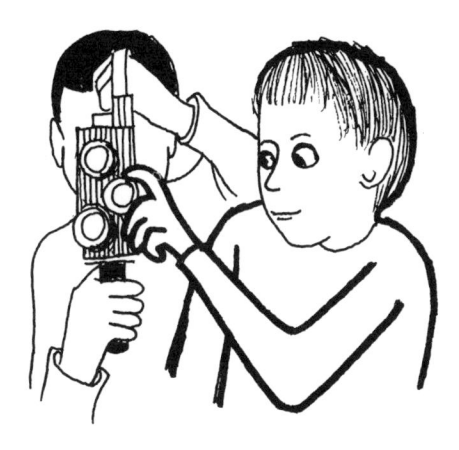

In moving shots, particularly from vehicles, you may want to increase the camera speed (frames per second) to smooth out any bumpiness. But remember, this slows the speed of action you are filming.

By the time you've reached the point of shooting, you have spent a lot of time, money, and energy. If you have any doubts about whether you have gotten the shot you want or not, take it again. It is simpler and cheaper than having to come back to do it over even if the shot is still there at another time.

YOU MIGHT MAKE A DOZEN TAKES OF A SINGLE SCENE

SCENE 6
TAKE 10

When you are shooting, start your camera at least three or four seconds before the action starts and keep the camera rolling for three or four seconds after the action is finished. This gives you footage to play with when you're editing. You will also need some extra frames if you are going to use a fade or a dissolve in that shot.

If you are following an action and you plan to have the action go out of frame, it's a good idea to frame a picture at the end and hold it even after the action has moved out of frame. Or sometimes you might move in to a close-up of some object in the frame after the action has moved out of frame. This can be helpful when you make transitions from shot to shot during editing. If you think ahead to the editing while you are shooting, you can make the editing a lot easier. Particularly if you are going to be the editor!

One of the techniques that has changed most about filming is the use of a great variety of camera angles. Do not be afraid to experiment with camera angles.

Another thing that has changed is the number of short shots that are used for telling a story. Make sure, when you are shooting, to cover your material in enough interesting ways to give yourself plenty of editing freedom.

THINGS TO REMEMBER IN ALL SHOOTING

Make a list of the equipment you will need each day. Check that you have everything and that each thing is working before you pack it.

Always carry enough batteries to cover the day's shooting. If your batteries are rechargeable, be sure to put them on charge at the end of each day's shooting.

If you are using a spring wind camera, remember to wind it after each shot.

Inspect and clean the gate of your camera after every roll to make sure that no dirt is there. Otherwise the dirt will be in your picture.

Make sure the lenses are clean and properly seated in the camera.

Never load your camera in the sun. When you reload a camera, do it quickly but not hurriedly. A jammed camera wastes time and film.

Make sure that your camera is set at the speed you want. If the camera has a tachometer, check the dial. If you have a speed dial (8, 16, 18, 24, 32 frames per second) and a footage counter, check the accuracy of the setting by timing it against the amount of film run.

AT THE BEGINNING OF EACH NEW ROLL, SHOOT AN IDENTIFYING SLATE

IN HAND-HELD FILMING, HOLD YOUR BREATH WHILE YOU ARE SHOOTING

WHAT IS A MOVING PICTURE?

In a moving picture the pictures don't really move. The only thing that moves is the film.

A film is a series of still pictures, each one a step in a complete motion. These pictures go by your eyes so quickly that they look like a continuous action. Your eyes do not work fast enough to see the spaces between the pictures. When the space between pictures comes along, you are still seeing the picture before it. You keep seeing that picture until a new one takes its place.

This is called *persistence of vision* and it is why moving pictures seem to move.

In the process of making a film a motion picture camera records a series of still pictures, focused by a lens, onto a roll of flexible, light-sensitive film that is moving through the camera in stops and starts.

When this film is chemically developed in a laboratory, the invisible pictures become visible.

Once film has been developed, it can be cut apart and rearranged in any way that best communicates the ideas of the filmmaker. This is called editing.

When the finished film is projected, it moves through the projector in stops and starts, usually at the same speed it moved through the camera. During the very short time that the film is moving from picture to picture, a shutter interrupts the brilliant projector light and the screen is black. When the film stops, the shutter moves out of the way and the image on the film is magnified and focused by a lens onto a screen for viewing.

WHAT SIZE ARE YOU GOING TO WORK IN?

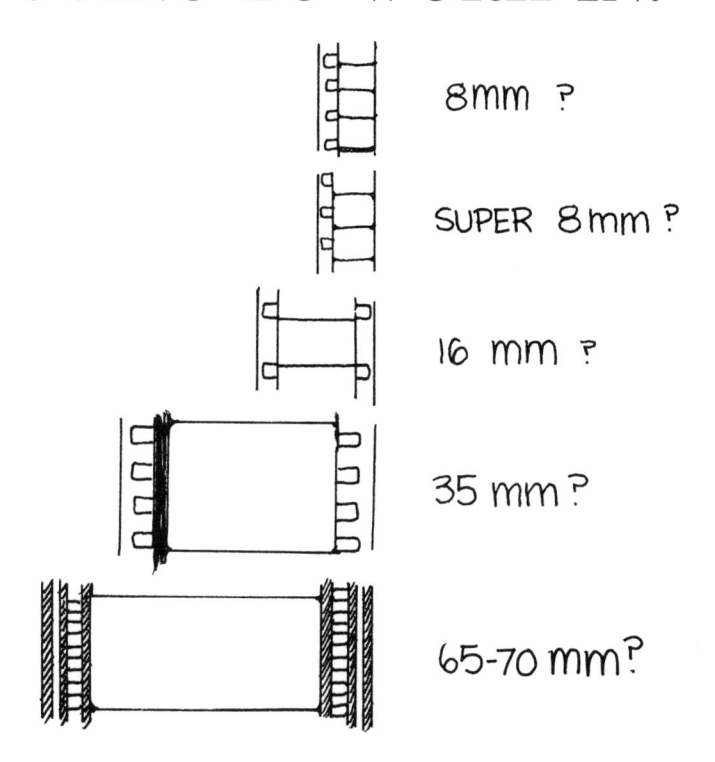

8mm?

SUPER 8mm?

16 mm?

35 mm?

65-70 mm?

Motion picture film is made in these five basic sizes. The size of film is measured in millimeters (mm).

65–70 mm and 35 mm are too expensive for noncommercial film making, so your choice will be between Super 8 mm, 8 mm, and 16 mm. Super 8 mm is replacing standard 8 mm film and cameras.

Super 8 mm should be the ideal noncommercial filmmaker's size. The cameras, accessories, and projectors are excellent. The cost of everything in 8 mm is much less than 16 mm.

Serious and excellent films are made in Super 8 mm. But all along the way, from the selection of raw film stock right up to the final projection, there are many choices that are open to 16 mm filmmakers that are not open to filmmakers working in Super 8 mm.

But, when you first start filming, ideas, concepts, style, and practice are the most important things, and using Super 8 mm won't hamper you at all.

CAMERAS

A camera is a light-tight box.

It has a lens (1) to focus the object being photographed onto the film.

It has a shutter (2), which keeps light from falling on the film when the film is moving, and lets the light through when the film is stopped.

It has a gate, which is made up of an aperture plate (3) and a pressure plate (4); the film moves between them. They keep the film flat and in place as each picture is taken.

It has a pull-down claw (5), that moves the film along, frame by frame, and holds it in place when the picture is being taken.

Sprocketed wheels (6) move the film along.

There is a viewfinder (7) for looking at the action while you are filming.

A footage counter (8) keeps track of the amount of film you've used.

A dial (9) is used to set the number of frames per second moving through the camera.

There is a spring wind or an electric motor to power the mechanism. All cameras have these features, even though some cameras are much more complicated.

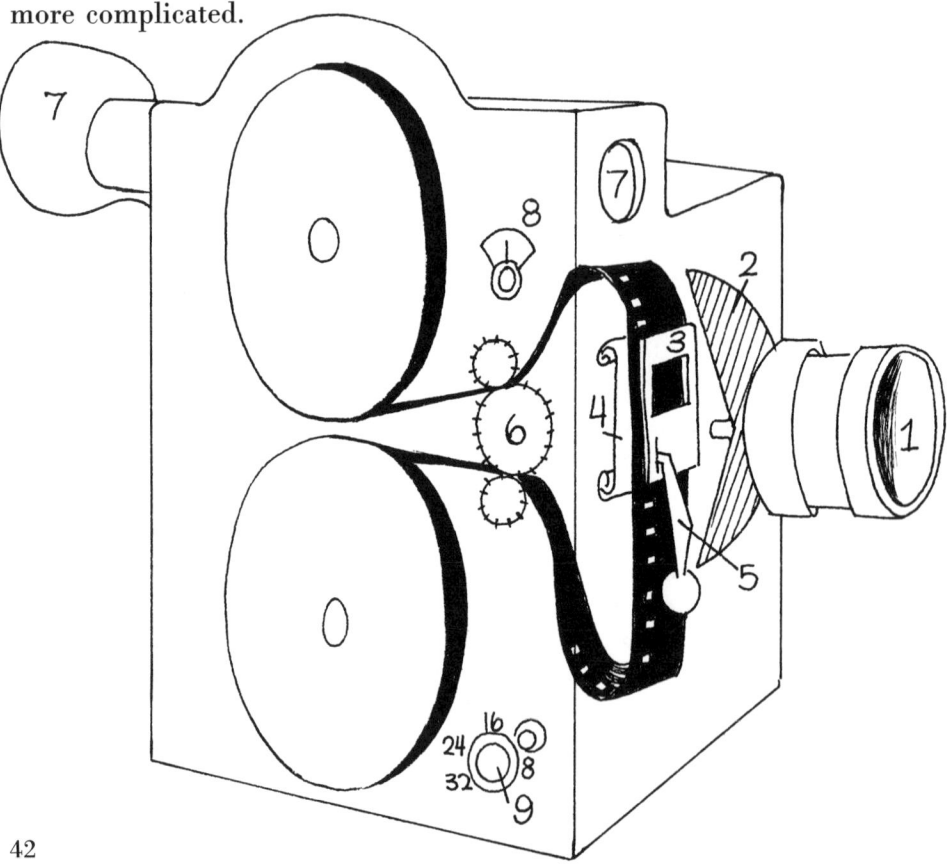

CHOOSING A CAMERA. WHAT KIND?

THE SUPER 8 MM CAMERA

The Super 8 mm camera is the simplest and least expensive camera for beginning filmmakers. It has many other advantages too.

It is light and easy to handle. Raw stock and development cost the least.

It has a factory-packed film cartridge for fast and easy loading. The cartridge can be changed at any time during filming, no matter how much or how little film has been used. Later the same cartridge can be put back into the camera and the remaining film used up.

This allows the cameraman to switch to a faster or slower film, or from black and white to color, or from outdoor color to indoor, artificial-light film. Any of these changes can be made quickly to fit filming needs with no loss of film.

FILM CARTRIDGE

There is a wide range of equipment available.

Projection equipment is less expensive than for other sizes.

Super 8 mm cameras range from very simple ones to sophisticated, professional cameras. Super 8 mm cameras may include these features:

Electric motor drive
Built-in exposure meter
Variable filming speeds
A zoom lens or even a motorized zoom
A reflex finder
Automatic exposure control
Synchronous sound

THIS SUPER 8mm CAMERA HAS MANY ADVANCED FEATURES, EVEN SYNCHRONOUS SOUND. IT IS EXCELLENT FOR ADVANCED HOME MOVIE MAKERS

Some Super 8 mm cameras may not have all of the automatic features but they may have features that are more important in advanced movie making, such as:

the ability to rewind film for intentional double exposures and special effects;

a variable shutter that allows fades and lap dissolves to be made in the camera;

accurate footage and frame counter, forward and reverse; single frame control for animation;

a multi-lens turret;

greater camera speed range.

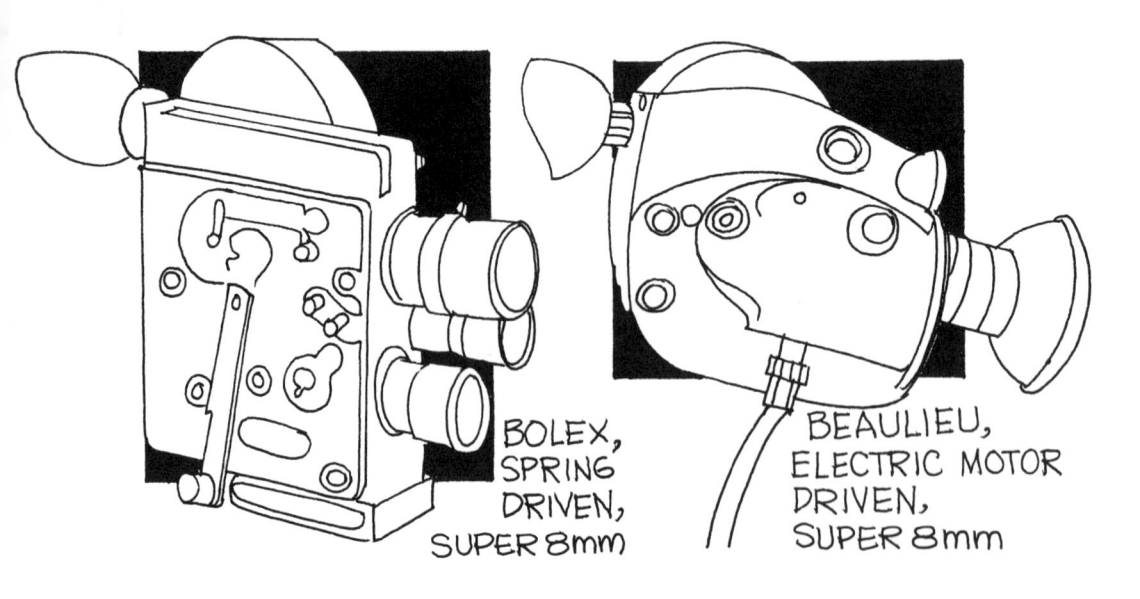

BOLEX, SPRING DRIVEN, SUPER 8mm

BEAULIEU, ELECTRIC MOTOR DRIVEN, SUPER 8mm

Super 8 mm has disadvantages too.

Very few types of film are made in Super 8 mm, although what is available is excellent.

Many laboratories do not handle Super 8 mm films at this time. Some may develop the film, but do not make prints.

It is difficult to have optical work done in Super 8 mm film. (When Super 8 mm is more widely used, this will change.) A few labs in the country make copies and do some optical work on Super 8 mm.

It is harder to edit Super 8 mm film. The small film size makes it harder to handle, and the small picture size makes it harder to see with the naked eye.

The picture on screen is small, which means smaller audiences. If the projection is too big, the picture is not as sharp.

BELL & HOWELL
16 mm
SPRING DRIVEN

SPRING WIND

THE 16 MM CAMERA

The 16 mm camera has become the most widely used professional size for all filming except major entertainment productions. Most documentaries, television news, industrial, scientific, and educational films are shot in 16 mm.

There are two basic kinds of 16 mm cameras:

1. Spring driven, 100 foot, daylight-load cameras.

2. External magazine cameras.

1. THE SPRING DRIVEN, DAYLIGHT-LOAD CAMERA

It is compact and light, so it is good for hand-held filming. It is reliable, rugged, and relatively cheap.

It is completely independent of batteries and electricity. (If you have an electrically powered camera, you must carry batteries and be able to recharge or replace them.) But if you want to, you can add an electric motor to some spring driven cameras.

These cameras can be loaded in daylight.

It is possible to get cheaper film in bulk and load your own daylight spools ahead of time in the darkroom.

The disadvantages of the spring driven camera are:

The longest scene that can be filmed without rewinding the spring is about 40 feet (slightly over one minute); this is with the most expensive of the spring winds.

It is limited to 100 foot film rolls.

It cannot be used for filming synchronous sound.

2. THE EXTERNAL MAGAZINE CAMERA

There are many kinds of external magazine 16 mm cameras. Most sound cameras are of this type. All are driven by electric motors.

In external magazine cameras the film is not stored in the camera box. It is loaded in a light-tight film magazine that attaches to the camera.

Magazines come in sizes that can hold 200, 400, 800, or 1200 foot rolls of film. This allows filming for a long time without stopping. The film is loaded into the magazine in a darkroom before going out to shoot or in a changing bag right on location. Usually a number of magazines are loaded ahead of time so that filming will not be held up when more film is needed.

It does not take long to change magazines on the camera, but it does take quite a while to load a magazine with film. Sometimes different kinds of film are loaded into different magazines to take care of changing situations during the day's shooting—a slow film and a fast film, or a daylight film and an artificial-light, indoor film. Magazines may be switched at any time, even in the middle of a roll.

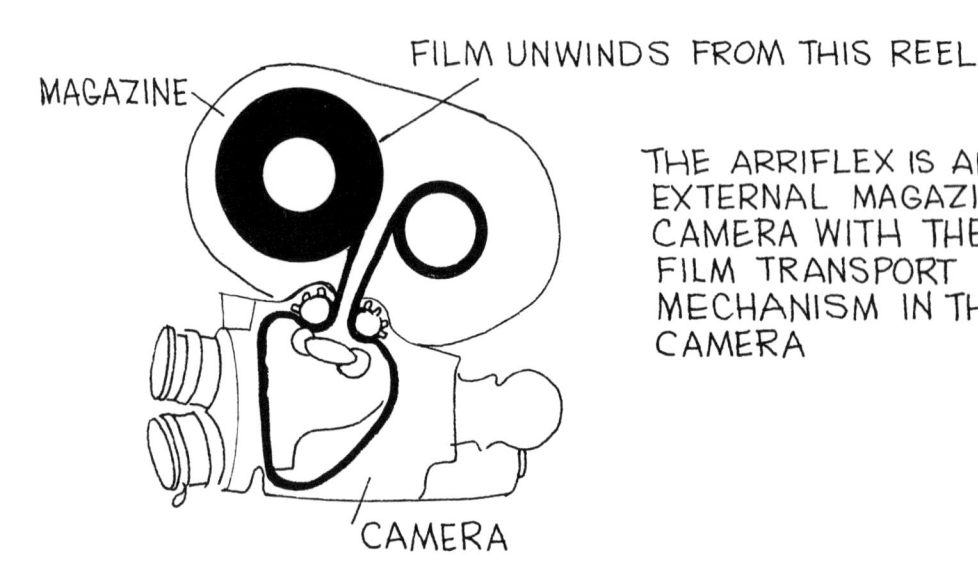

MAGAZINE

FILM UNWINDS FROM THIS REEL

THE ARRIFLEX IS AN EXTERNAL MAGAZINE CAMERA WITH THE FILM TRANSPORT MECHANISM IN THE CAMERA

CAMERA

There are two kinds of magazines. One is just a box for the film to feed out of, and back into, after it has been exposed in the camera. Most of the mechanism is in the camera itself. The film is threaded from the magazine, through the camera, and back into the magazine.

FILM FEEDS FROM A CHAMBER IN THE OTHER SIDE OF THE MAGAZINE

FILM TAKE-UP SIDE

THE ECLAIR IS AN EXTERNAL MAGAZINE CAMERA WITH THE FILM TRANSPORT MECHANISM IN THE MAGAZINE

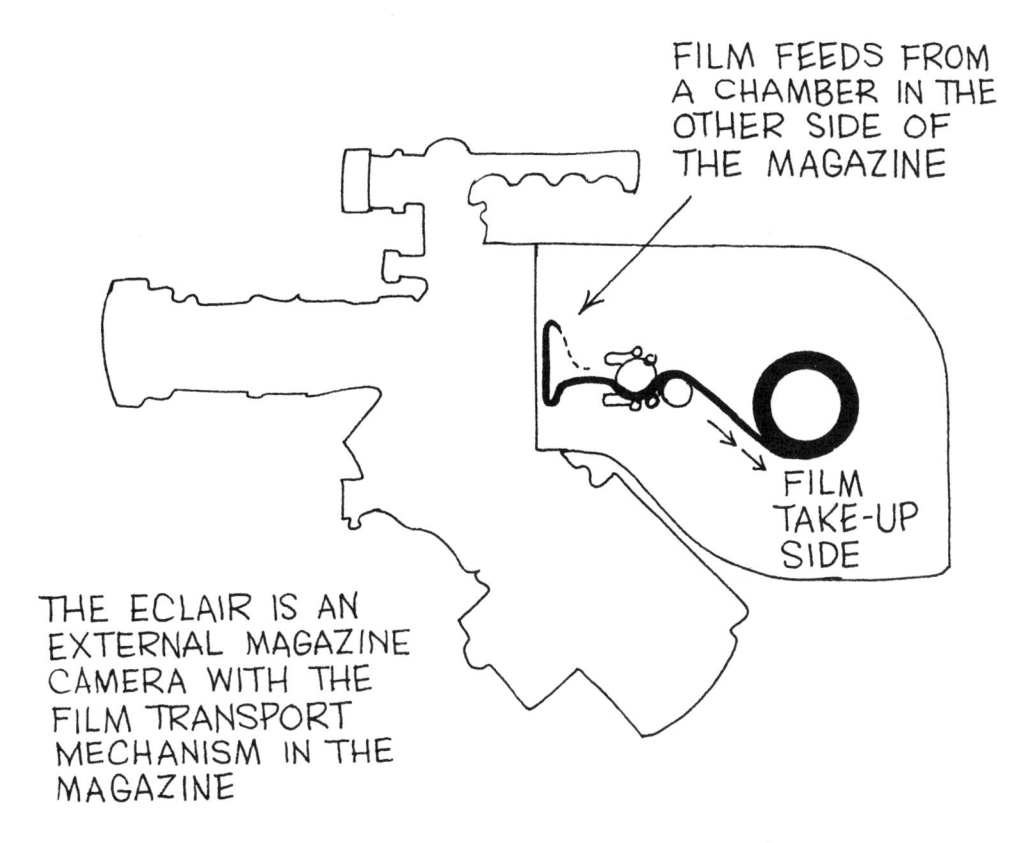

In the other kind, much of the mechanism for moving the film is in the magazine, which just clips onto the camera box. The film does not have to be threaded. This makes it easy and quick to change magazines. But magazines like this are very expensive.

External magazine cameras are used in sound filming because they allow for longer scenes.

THOMAS EDISON INVENTED THE MOTION PICTURE CAMERA

SPRING DRIVEN EDISON CAMERA, 1902

LENSES

The lens is the eye of your camera.

The quality of your lens determines the sharpness and brightness of your pictures.

The focal length and speed of a lens determine where, when, and how you shoot any sequence.

Focal Length

The focal length of a lens determines the size of the picture you are going to get on your film from any particular distance. Lenses that cannot change their focal length are called fixed focal length lenses. The focal length of a lens is measured either in millimeters (mm) or inches.

SHORT FOCAL LENGTH LENS   LONG FOCAL LENGTH LENS
(THE CAMERA IS IN THE SAME PLACE IN BOTH SHOTS)

The shorter the focal length of a lens, the wider the angle of the picture will be, and the smaller everything in the picture will be. The longer the lens, the narrower the angle of the picture will be; yet everything in the picture will be larger.

There is a "normal" lens for each size film. When you want more in the picture, use a wide-angle lens. When you want to bring something closer or make it larger, use a long focal length, or a telephoto lens.

See the table on p. 91 for some examples of the approximate focal length lenses to use with various film sizes to get normal, wide-angle, or telephoto pictures.

Zoom Lenses

A zoom lens has an adjustment that changes its focal length. It can change from a wide-angle lens, to a normal lens, to a long focal length lens, even while the camera is running. Because of this, a zoom lens allows the cameraman to change the picture size of something without moving the camera nearer, or farther away, from the object. Without moving, he can go smoothly from a wide shot to a close-up. Or he can go the other way.

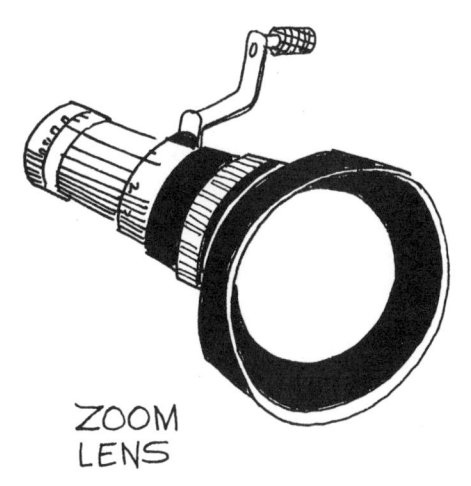

ZOOM LENS

ORIGINAL PICTURE

IF YOU ZOOM IN, THE SUBJECT JUST GETS LARGER

IF YOU MOVE IN, THE PERSPECTIVE CHANGES TOO

The zoom makes "moving" very easy. But the effect on the screen of a zoom shot is not quite the same as when the camera itself is moved. When the camera is moved, the object seems to stay where it is and the audience does the moving. In a zoom shot, the object seems to move closer or farther away. Make sure you know which effect you want.

By zooming the lens, and so changing its focal length, you can keep the thing you are filming the same size on the screen, even if it is moving toward or away from the camera.

Always focus a zoom lens wide open, in its longest focal length position. Then adjust it back to the focal length you want to use.

A disadvantage of the zoom lens is that generally it is not as fast as a set focal length lens. You need more light to use it.

Many zoom lenses have motors that zoom them in and out smoothly and at various speeds. The zoom lens is by all odds the most versitile lens to start with, if you can afford it.

There are also auxiliary lenses that can be attached to a zoom lens to make it a longer telephoto lens or better for very close filming.

Speed

The speed of a lens tells the maximum amount of light it allows through onto the film. The more light a lens lets through, the faster it is.

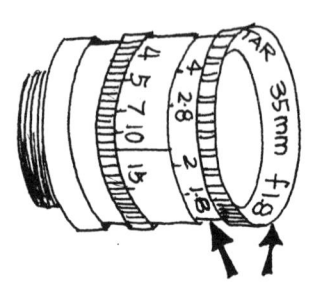

This speed is indicated by an f stop number. The f number of a lens always indicates its fastest speed. You can have an f 1.2, or f 1.9, or f 2.8, or f 3.5 lens.

The smaller the f number, the more light the lens lets through, and the faster the lens is. An f 1.2 lens is faster than an f 2.8, and f 2.8 is faster than an f 3.5.

THE SPEED OF A LENS APPEARS ON THE LENS RIM AND AS THE LOWEST f STOP NUMBER

All lenses that have the same f number have the same speed, even though they may have different focal lengths. They let the same amount of light through. Generally the faster the lens for any focal length, the more expensive the lens is.

The speed of your lens dictates whether or not you have enough light in any scene to get a proper exposure. It determines whether you have to wait for the sun to get out from behind the cloud, or wait until tomorrow to film, or not be able to shoot inside. It determines whether you have to move the subject into the sunlight, or add lights, or change films, or change the number of frames per second that you are shooting at.

IF YOU HAVE A SLOW LENS, YOU CAN TAKE THE PICTURE IN THE SUN BUT NOT THE ONE IN THE SHADOW

Almost all camera lenses have a movable iris that can be opened up or made smaller to control the amount of light coming through. This opening is called the aperture.

Apertures are worked out on a graduated scale. Each size opening is marked with an f stop number. The smallest f number shows the basic speed of the lens. At that number the iris is wide open, letting through all the light that a particular lens can let through. The wide open f stop number is the same as the f stop number of the lens itself.

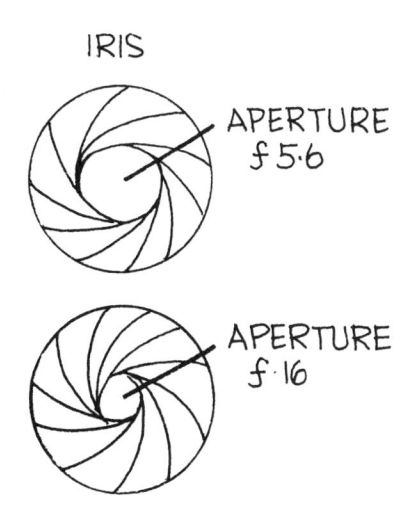

IRIS

APERTURE f 5·6

APERTURE f·16

The next opening on the scale allows only half as much light through. Each smaller opening allows half as much light through as the one before it. The f stops on a typical lens might be: f 2, 2.8, 4, 5.6, 8, 11, 16, 22, 32. So a setting of f 4 allows through half as much light as f 2.8. f 2.8 lets twice as much light through as f 4. Exposure is controlled primarily by changing the f stops.

Take care of your lenses. Keep them covered with lens caps when you are not using them. When lenses are off the camera, cover them at both ends.

Use only lens tissue to clean a lens. Use a rubber air bulb before and after you use the tissue.

Dry and clean your lens as soon as possible after using it in bad weather.

Don't let a lens sit in the hot sun for any length of time.

It is a good idea to have your lens checked every so often to be sure that it is optically correct and that the f stops have not changed. (This can happen if the lens is jarred or dropped.)

LENS

ALWAYS USE A SUNSHADE

IF A FILTER IS NEEDED, MOUNT IT BETWEEN THE LENS AND THE SUNSHADE

FILMING ACCESSORIES

These are good and necessary accessories to all-around filming.

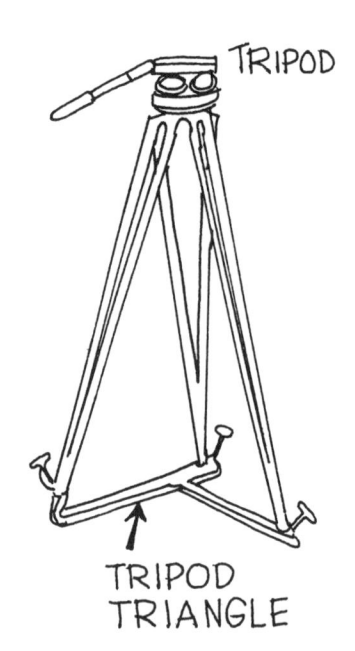

A tripod. Either a good friction head or, even better, a fluid head tripod. The fluid head is smoother, but generally more expensive. This can have a ball joint leveling device that allows you to level the camera without changing the position of the tripod legs. A good tripod can cost more than a camera. Get the best one you can afford.

A tripod triangle keeps tripod legs from slipping on a smooth surface.

An exposure meter. Even if your camera has a built-in meter, it is a good idea to have a separate exposure meter to check against the one in the camera. You also need a separate meter if you are going to work with lights.

A case for your equipment is convenient and protective. A rigid case is best.

A matte box is a combination filter holder and lens shade that attaches to the camera and fits different sized lenses.

A camera body brace helps to hold a heavy camera steady when it is hand held.

A lens shade keeps the direct rays of the sun from hitting the lens.

Filters for correcting color film when used in different kinds of light or for getting specific effects either in black and white or color.

A viewing filter for looking at the sun to see if it is going behind clouds or coming out. Never look at the sun without it. Also for checking the range of contrast in a scene.

Extra batteries for the camera.

A film slate is a board on which you can write identifying information: production name, location, scene number, take number, date, director's and cameraman's name. This slate is photographed for a few seconds, as needed in each reel. A sound slate, or "sticks," also has a hinged piece of wood that is clapped at the beginning of every sound take. This is one method of putting the picture and sound track in sync when you start editing.

Ink markers for writing on cans, tape, or slates.

Chalk for marking positions.

Empty film cans so that if only part of a roll of film is exposed, that exposed part can be sent to the lab.

Camera tape is used for taping up a film can after the exposed film has been put in; for taping several cans together; and for taping instructions onto the package.

Gaffer tape is indispensable to any production. It can patch up any equipment, stick anything to anything, and hang anything anywhere.

Lens cleaning tissues and air bulb. Do not use a brush to clean your lens. It leaves oil and bristles. Blow away loose dust with the air bulb, wipe with the tissues, then blow again.

A few small tools: a pliers, different sizes of screwdrivers (including a Phillips), emery cloth, graphite and oil lubricators, tweezers, fine file, wooden manicure sticks for scraping emulsion from the gate.

A CAMERAMAN KEEPS AN ASSORTMENT OF EMERGENCY ODDS AND ENDS IN HIS "DITTY BOX"

FILM

One side of film is coated with light-sensitive emulsion. (This is the dull side.) Unexposed film is called raw stock. Knowing about film is one of the most complicated, and technical parts of filming.

All films have certain characteristics.

They have a *speed* which shows how sensitive the film is to light. The speed of the film is given as a number on a special scale. The number is called the ASA exposure index. The higher the number, the faster (or more sensitive to light) the film is. A film rated 100 ASA is twice as fast as a film rated 50 ASA. All films have two ASA index numbers. One tells how fast the film is in daylight, and the other, how fast it is in artificial light.

When there is not much light, you can either add light or use a faster film. You will get a better picture if you add light, but this may be expensive, impossible, or destroy the reality of the scene.

The faster a film is, the grainier it is. *Grain* is another characteristic of film.

Grain relates to the size of the chemical particles that make up the emulsion of a film. The grainier the picture is, the less sharp it is, and the poorer the quality of the picture, either in color or black and white.

Incorrect exposure makes a picture grainier.

Too long developing makes a picture grainier.

Another characteristic of film is *contrast*, or latitude. This refers to the range of tones between very dark and very light on the film. Color films have color tone too.

GEORGE EASTMAN INVENTED THE FIRST FLEXIBLE ROLL FILM IN 1884, AND THE ROLL HOLDER FOR WINDING IT

TYPES OF FILM

Whether they are black and white or color, there are two types of films, reversal and negative.

When you use a reversal film you usually project the same film that went through your camera. A reversal film has no negative, but you can make copies of it. Almost all Super 8 mm films are reversal films. In 16 mm you can get either reversal or negative film.

A negative film is used only in the camera. A print is made from the developed negative, and that print is used in the projector.

A great deal of 16 mm work is done with reversal film, particularly in color. Many filmmakers work with reversal film as if they were using a negative. A work print is made from the original reversal film, and that work print is edited. Then the original reversal film is cut to match the work print, and prints are made from that original. (See Editing, Processing)

CHOOSING THE RIGHT FILM

There are many, many kinds and types of film. They are different in their sensitivity to light and color, their speed, grain, contrast, and the way they react to developing. They are even different in the number of sprocket holes they have and the ways they are wound on film spools and packed. It is almost impossible for a filmmaker to get to know everything about every kind of film.

But while you are working in Super 8 mm, you don't really have this problem. There are fewer films available. Some of these are:

In black and white:

Eastman Kodak Plus X, rated ASA 50 daylight, 40 tungsten. Plus X is a fine grain, medium fast film and is good for general outdoor filming or where you have plenty of artificial light. It has good contrast.

Eastman Kodak Tri X, ASA 200 daylight, 160 tungsten. Tri X is a high speed film for general interior filming. It can also be used outside when the light is poor.

In color:

Eastman Kodak Kodachrome II, ASA daylight, 24 (with no. 85 filter) and ASA 40 with photoflood or 3400K (see p. 57). Kodachrome II is excellent for outdoor use and does not require to much light if you use it inside. Eastman makes copies from this film.

Agfa-Gevaert Agfacolor 2540, ASA 25 daylight, 40 tungsten. This is also a good all-around color film.

In 16 mm the choice is so wide that there is a film to fit almost any condition you could be filming under. Just remember that in selecting a film you have to consider all the characteristics and decide which ones will achieve what you want in your film. You may have to decide between speed and graininess, or speed and color quality, or contrast and print quality.

If you are working in 16 mm, read specification sheets, talk to your film-making friends, and experiment yourself until you find a few films that are good under different conditions. Then use those films regularly. You will get to know how they work and what you have to do to get the results you want with them.

Film is perishable. It must be stored in a cool, dry place. Some professionals store their film in a refrigerator.

Film goes out of date. When you buy film, look at the date to be sure it has a long time to go before it expires. If you have any amount of film, use the film with the earliest expiration date first. Outdated film can still be good and it is cheap. Don't use it for important sequences, but it is fine to practice and experiment with. Be sure to test a roll of it before buying any amount.

Film is manufactured in batches, and each batch varies a little. Each batch has its own emulsion number. If you are doing a big production with a lot of film, check to be sure it all has the same emulsion number.

HAVE FILM DEVELOPED AS SOON AS POSSIBLE

LIGHTING

You must have enough light to expose your film properly. Enough light to your eyes is not always enough light to get a picture. How much light you need, and what kind of light, depends on your lens, the camera speed, and the kind and speed of film you are using. Black and white film is available in much faster speeds than color.

With black and white film, the kind of light doesn't matter too much as long as it is bright enough to give you an image. With color film, not only must the light be bright enough, but it must be proper color. In daylight that means don't film too early in the morning or too late in the afternoon, unless you are after early morning or late afternoon effects. The color of light changes during the day. At those times it gets very red or yellow, and you won't be able to match pictures you take then with pictures you take during the rest of the day.

When you use artificial light, use only enough to give a proper exposure and make things look natural. Lights are used outside when there is not enough daylight, or to fill in the shadow side of a scene with high contrast.

New lighting equipment is small, portable, and efficient. The development of the quartz lamp has been a big help. Quartz light is very intense, does not draw much current, and is the proper color temperature, between 3200° and 3400° Kelvin. (The Kelvin scale is used to measure color, which has a temperature just as heat does.)

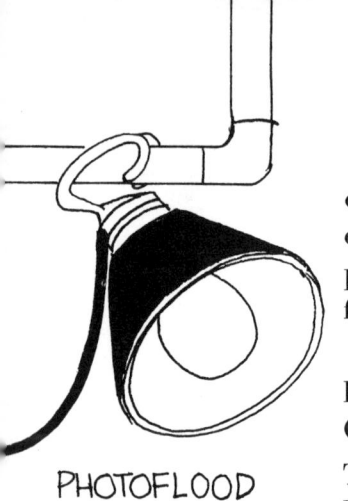

PHOTOFLOOD BULBS FIT INTO ANY FIXTURE

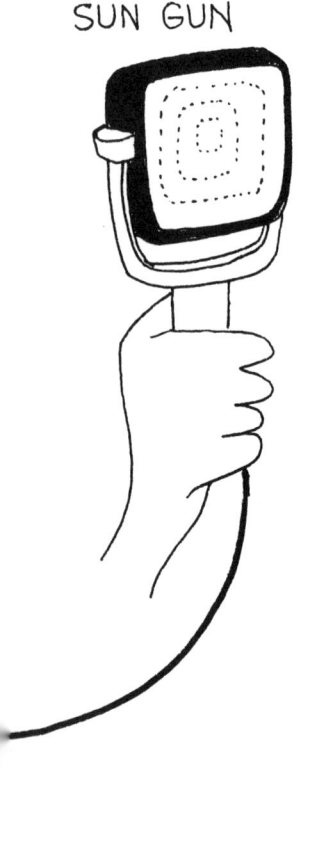

SUN GUN

It is general practice to own a few basic lights and rent others to meet the requirements of different jobs. The least expensive lighting equipment for simple productions is the photoflood bulb which can be used in almost any kind of fixture and reflector. Photofloods are corrected for color.

Lighting units come in many forms for different purposes. Here are some:

Colortran Quartz lights are compact and very effective.

The Lowel-light is another compact, handy light. It can be mounted almost anywhere with gaffer tape.

A Sun gun light is a portable light which operates on rechargeable batteries. It is indispensable if you are going to work somewhere without a light plug. Sun guns are necessary if you are shooting in a car, plane, boat, or any other moving vehicle. But they only burn for ten minutes without recharging.

Another handy lighting device is the umbrella light, which gives a good diffused light so that a scene looks natural.

A piece of lighting equipment that is useful when you are filming outdoors is a reflector. You can buy a reflector or make one with aluminum foil.

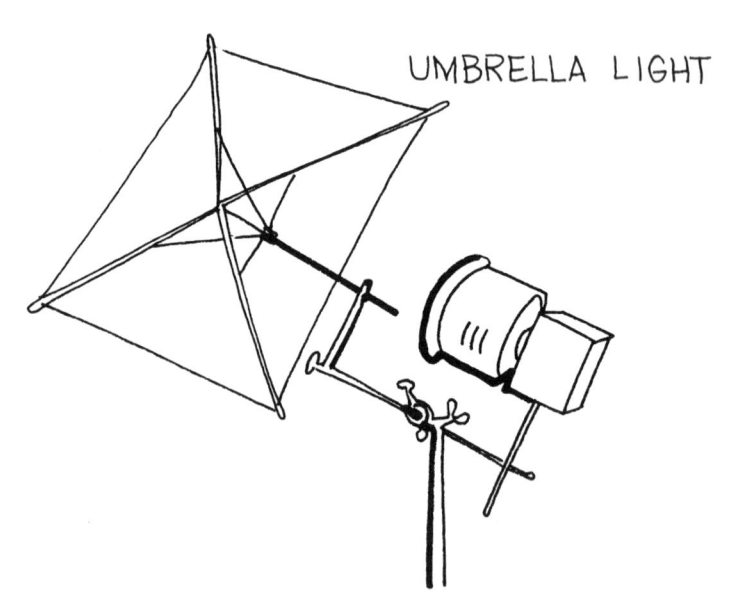

UMBRELLA LIGHT

REFLECTORS

A reflector reflects the sun's light onto the shadow side of the subject so the contrast isn't too great and you see detail in the shadows.

The function of lighting, once you have enough light for exposure, is to emphasize and give character to the important things and people in the picture, no matter where they move in the scene. But remember, every light you use makes a shadow and too many shadows spoil a picture.

Lighting creates mood. Dark, shadowy lighting gives a feeling of gloom, danger, suspense, tragedy. Bright, high-key lighting is cheerful, gay, safe. Make sure that the kind of lighting you use is not in conflict with the mood of your story.

Here are some other common lights used in filming.

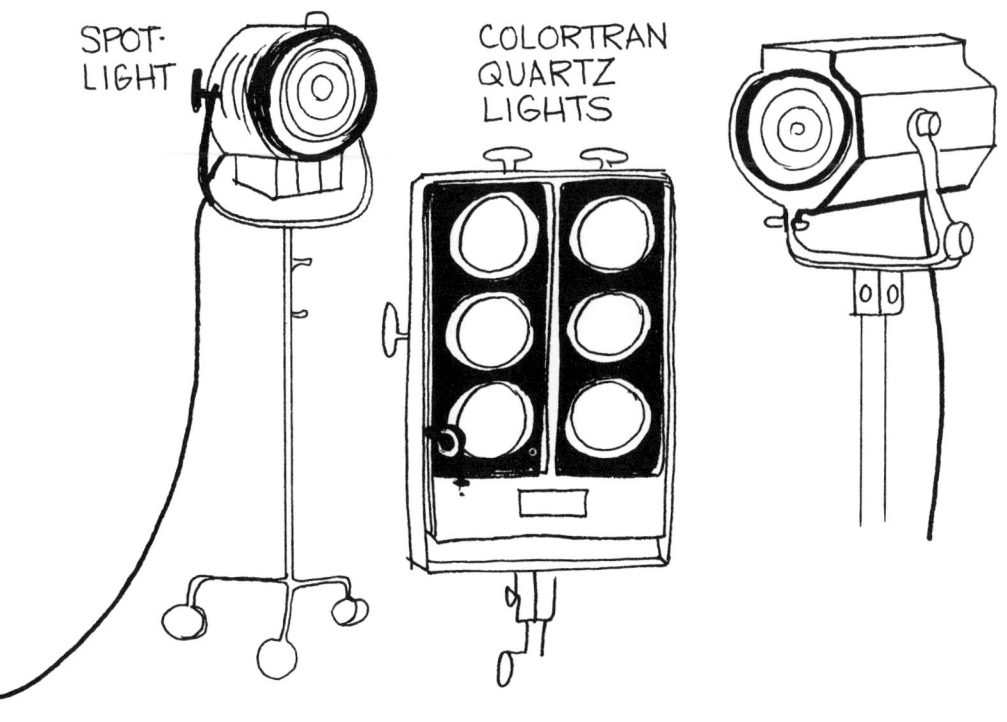

SPOTLIGHT

COLORTRAN QUARTZ LIGHTS

SOUND

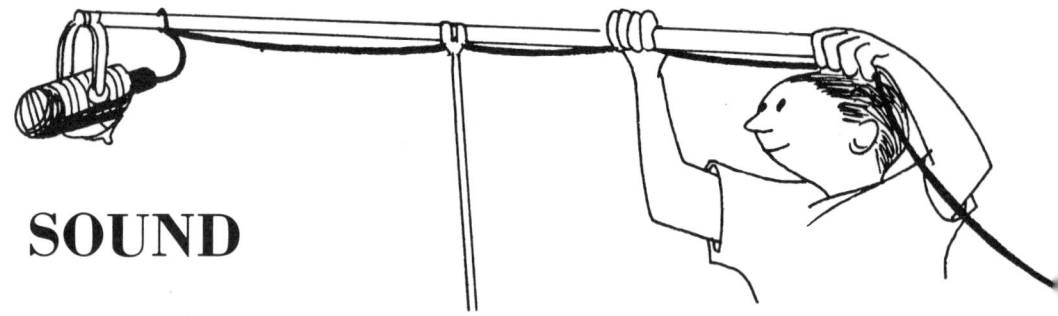

Sound adds another dimension to your film. Sound makes things more real. People speak in their own voices. Noises make a place come alive. Music sets a mood. You can communicate your ideas better with pictures and sound than with pictures alone.

In film work there are two kinds of sound—optical and magnetic.

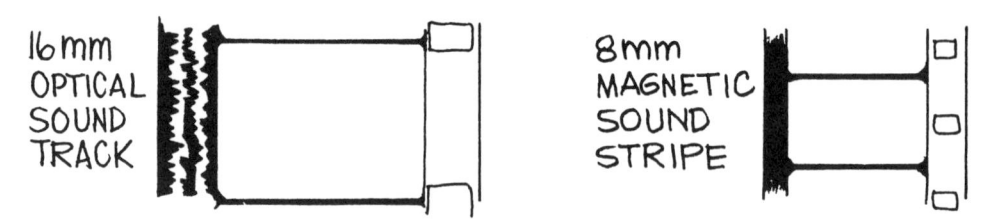

16mm OPTICAL SOUND TRACK

8mm MAGNETIC SOUND STRIPE

Optical sound is recorded on film by means of a light source that varies as the sound changes.

Magnetic sound is electronically recorded on magnetic tape. Almost all film sound is recorded magnetically. On the finished film it may be on a magnetic, or an optical, track.

There are two basic methods of recording.

Synchronous (or "sync") sound is recorded at the same time the picture is being filmed. The camera and the sound recorder are run precisely together. Every frame of film has its own corresponding sound. But shooting synchronous sound is complicated and expensive.

To shoot "sync" sound you need:
    a sync camera and a sync recorder;
    at least one microphone;

If you are inside, you have to shoot in a sound proof studio. If you are outside, on location, you have to be sure that other noises don't interfere with your sound.

Laboratory work and editing are both much more complicated and more expensive when sync sound is involved. Unless you are filming direct dialog, where you hear what people are saying and watch their lips at the same time, you really don't need it.

Non-synchronous sound is recorded separately from the picture and added to the film later.

To do this you need a tape recorder. There are two kinds of magnetic tape recorders, the ¼-inch reel machine and the cassette recorder. Both kinds can record with excellent quality. Many models of both kinds are portable and run on batteries. But if you have to make a choice of one machine to use in producing sound film, choose the ¼-inch machine.

¼-Inch Tape Recorder

1. The ¼-inch can run at various speeds, 1⅞, 3¾, 7½ inches per second. This allows you to make choices between the length of time you need and the quality.

2. Can be edited.

3. ¼-inch tape is the professional standard, and all music and effects are available in ¼-inch.

4. Sound studio equipment is based on ¼-inch so that if you need help they can handle your material.

5. Allows you to create effects by recording at one speed and playing back at another.

6. The tape is cheaper per minute.

Cassette Recorder

The cassette has only a single speed.
The advantage of a cassette is its small size and ease of handling.

Cannot be edited.

Cannot create effects.

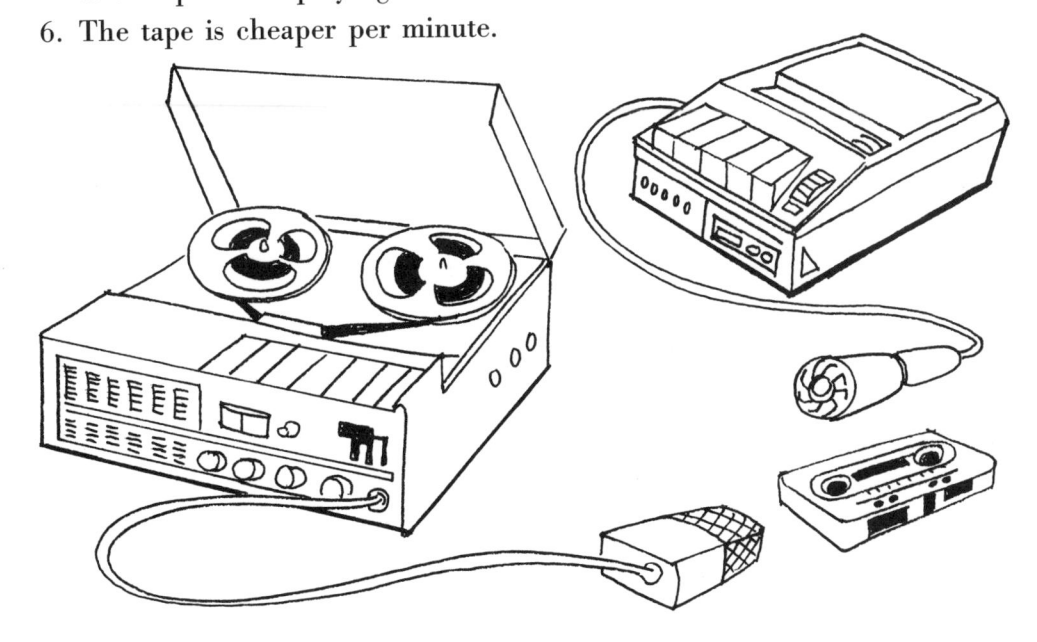

At every location bring along your tape recorder and record the sounds of the place. This is called "wild sound"—crowd and traffic noises, animal sounds, and even the comments of the people in the scene. If you are a one-man crew, you can do this before or after you film your pictures. But don't wait too long, because the sounds of a location change. A rush hour sounds different from a nonrush hour. Feeding time at the zoo doesn't sound like sleeping time.

Sometimes you might record your sound first and use it as a shooting outline. For example, you might record children talking about their neighborhood, then use that as a guide for showing the neighborhood.

After the film has been edited, if you are going to have a narration, first make a scene by scene "shot list." Write down the running time of each scene. Then write a narration to match your film. Timing is very important. You can't have a long speech over a short scene. Have the narrator rehearse with the projected film running at the proper speed.

PICTURE	TIME	SOUND
Leaves falling	6 secs.	Narration for this scene can only last 6 seconds. (Time it to be sure.)

Don't try to record the narration in the same room with the projector running, or you will pick up the sound of the projector. Record the narration, sequence by sequence, in a quiet place. You don't have to record the whole thing at one time.

You can also record music or background sounds from a record or an instrument while you record the narration. Sound effects records may be bought.

Use a single microphone, but experiment, first, with the narrator and the background sounds at different distances from it to be sure that the sounds don't interfere with each other. Make a test recording to check.

Another way is to record the narration on one tape and the music or effects on another. Then you can mix them on a third tape. Do it like this:

Put the narration track on one machine.

Put the music track on another.

Put unrecorded tape on a third machine.

Connect the output of the narration and music recorders into the mixer, and the output of the mixer into the third tape recorder. Start the three machines, balance the sound, and record.

If a mixer is not available, then set the narration and music tapes on "play," and the third machine (with its microphone attached) on "record." Start all three machines together and record through the open mike.

TAPE RECORDER RECORDING

NARRATION

TAPE RECORDER ON "PLAY"

MUSIC

TAPE RECORDER ON "PLAY"

MIKE

Except for what you are recording, the room must be absolutely quiet. The microphone will even pick up the sound of a clock ticking.

After this mixing, you will end up with a single tape. Then, when you are showing your film, set up the projector and the tape recorder and start them together. They should stay pretty much in sync throughout the showing.

A more exact and permanent method of adding sound is to have a magnetic stripe put on your finished picture film and rerecord your mixed sound track on that.

This can be done by using a magnetic sound projector as a magnetic recorder. Most magnetic sound projectors can record this way.

Put your mixed tape on a tape recorder.

Feed the output of the tape recorder into the recording unit of the projector. Be sure to start the tape machine and the projector exactly together so that the sound and picture are in sync on your film.

In Super 8 mm, record sound at either 24 or 18 frames per second, depending on the speed at which you shot your film. In 16mm, record your sound at 24 frames per second.

TITLES AND CREDITS

Titles and credits help set the mood of the film. They should be in the same style as the film.

You have seen many kinds of titles at the movies. Many of these can be done with simple animation, or double exposure, or stop action, or upside down camera work.

You can use original art work for your titles. You can cut out letters from papers or magazines. You can buy letters and assemble them into your title. You can use a crawl.

YOU CAN MAKE A CRAWL OUT OF SHELF PAPER AND AN OLD SHADE ROLLER. FILM THE LETTERING AS IT ROLLS BY

PRODUCED AND DIRECTED BY
EVAN SANCHEZ

CAMERAMAN
LARRY GARI

WRITER
KAREN BEE

GRIPS
LUKE GEFF
ADAM JOSH

SPONSORS
JOE'S SPORTS STORE
MAX'S DINER
STOP 'N' SHOP
AND
THE KIRBY CINEMA

But the most important ingredient in making titles is imagination. If you have the idea, you can usually figure out a way to do it.

Screen recognition for talent and jobs well done, and to say "thank you," may be all the pay the crew, actors, and sponsors get. Screen credit is a great morale builder and a possible substitute for cash.

ANIMATION

An animated film makes things that can't move look as if they are moving. This is done by filming pictures frame by frame, as the animator changes the action a little bit between each frame. The more frames used to complete the action, the smoother the action is. The finished film is projected at normal speed. If normal speed is 18 frames per second, you must shoot 18 single pictures for every second of screen time.

Animation is effective and good fun. It can be inexpensive. Some kinds of animation can tell a great deal in a very short time. It is also a good way to show clearly how things work.

There are many kinds of animation. The most expensive and difficult is cell animation. This is done by making many drawings of an action with each drawing (or cell) advancing the movement a little bit. Each drawing is filmed on a single frame. Animated cartoons are made like this. So are animated diagrams.

Simpler, but very good, animations can be made by using cutout figures in different stages of movement. Figures are substituted for each other in each new frame. As many figures as you want can be used, and used over and over, to complete an action. These figures can be drawings or photographs.

USE A DRAWING OR PHOTOGRAPH AS BACKGROUND.
MOVE THE FIGURE ACROSS THE SCENE

Modeling clay or plasticene figures are good for animations because you can change their position after each frame. Jointed figures are easy to manipulate too.

Any real thing like a box or a pencil appears to move if you change its position from frame to frame.

If you have two cameras and are working with three-dimensional objects, you can get two angles of any animated action by exposing a frame on each camera after each move. By editing the two angles, you get greater variety and more screen time with the same amount of manipulation.

Animation can be done with any camera that has a mechanism for making single frame exposures. This is an important thing to look for when buying a camera. When you are making single frame exposures, be sure to check the shutter speed so you can figure out what your exposure should be. It varies greatly in different cameras.

All animation must be done with the camera on a tripod or some kind of animation stand.

If you plan to animate to any kind of sound track, time the segments of sound and figure out how many frames of action you need to match a segment. Keep in mind the speed at which you are going to project.

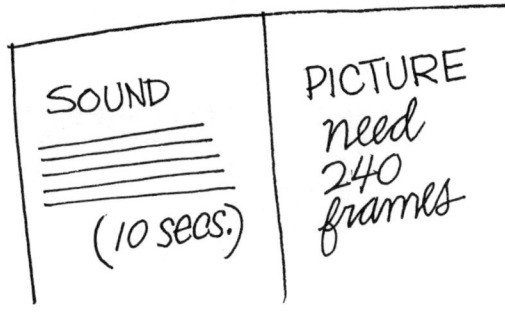

SOUND	PICTURE
≡≡≡≡ (10 secs.)	need 240 frames

Another way of giving movement to things that don't move, such as drawings, paintings, and still photographs, is to film these things at normal speed with a moving camera. You can zoom in or out on details of a picture, pan across, or up and down. With this technique you can enliven materials that might otherwise be static and uninteresting. Sometimes very fast cutting is used with this to make it even livelier.

With animation you can create great fantasy adventures, do many kinds of comedy, and be as outlandish as your imagination allows.

YOU CAN USE TYPING PAPER. MAKE A BOTTOM FRAME SO THE PICTURES ARE ALWAYS IN EXACTLY THE SAME PLACE ON THE STAND

YOU CAN BUY PUNCHED ANIMATION PAPER AND THE PEGS TO SLIP IT ON

ANIMATION STANDS

PROCESSING

A laboratory develops your original film.

When you send film to the laboratory, send along this information with it: what kind of film it is; how much film there is; whether you want it developed normally or given special processing; if you want a print and what kind.

A laboratory can correct some of the problems you may have had with exposure if they know about them before they process the film. If you have had to work in poor light, tell the lab that the picture is underexposed, and how much, and ask them to "push" the development, which means to develop the film longer than they normally would.

If you order it, a lab can:

1. Make a one-light work print from either negative or reversal film. A one-light work print means that there are no corrections in the printing. You can also get a corrected work print, but this is expensive.

You can get these work prints in black and white or color.

If you are going to edit a work print, tell the lab that you want the edge numbers of the original printed through on your work print. You can use these numbers to identify scenes on your original when you cut it to match your edited work print.

2. Make answer prints from your edited original.

3. Make release prints.

4. Do optical effects—fades and dissolves.

5. Make optical sound tracks from magnetic tracks.

There are many other things a lab can do when they make prints for release.

If you are working in Super 8 mm, film is usually returned for processing to the company that made the film. Many labs handle 16 mm film.

If the film is to be returned to you by mail or express, be sure it has your return address.

Optical Effects

If you want any optical effects besides fades and dissolves, such as superimpositions, frame enlargements, trick effects, they will have to be done in the camera or at an optical printing house.

Restoring Film

If your original film becomes badly scratched and dirty during editing, there are places where you can have some of the damage repaired. This is a good idea if you are going to have prints made from that original.

If you have any problems with your film other than creative ones, don't hesitate to get in touch with the various processing houses. They are usually happy to help.

FADE OUT

FADE IN

GEORGE MELIES, IN 1897, ACCIDENTALLY DISCOVERED THE FADE OUT. THEN, EXPERIMENTING, HE DISCOVERED THE FADE IN, DISSOLVE, DOUBLE EXPOSURE, SLOW MOTION AND FAST MOTION PHOTOGRAPHY

EDITING

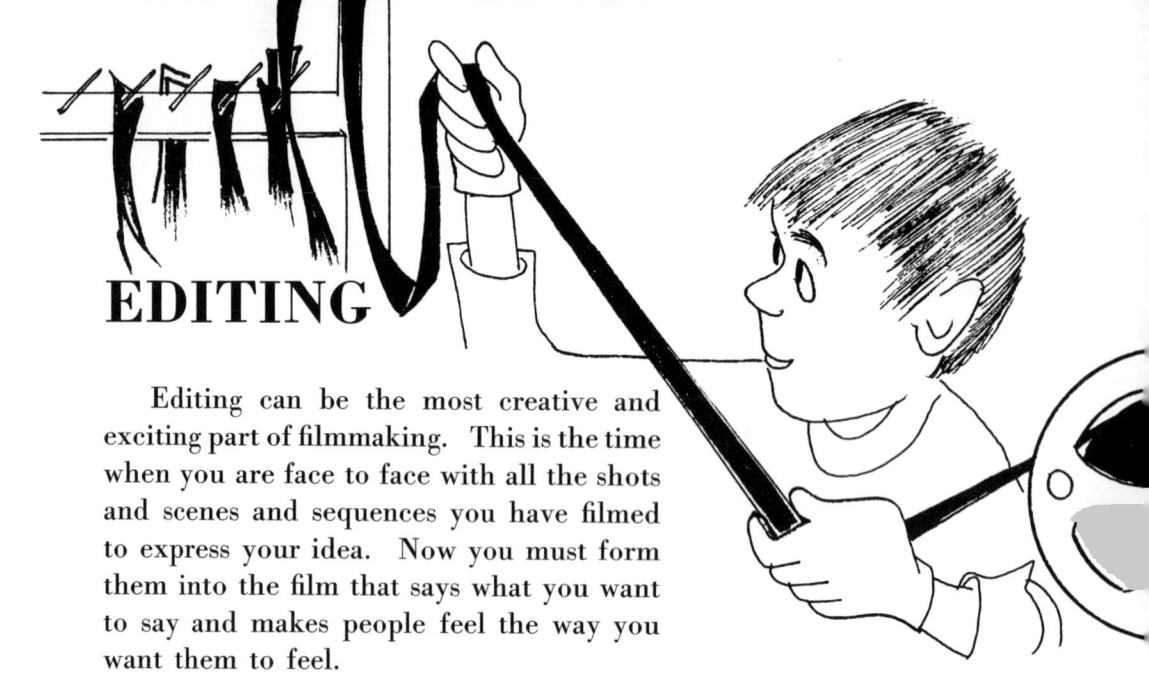

Editing can be the most creative and exciting part of filmmaking. This is the time when you are face to face with all the shots and scenes and sequences you have filmed to express your idea. Now you must form them into the film that says what you want to say and makes people feel the way you want them to feel.

Nowhere in the whole film making process is there a better place to experiment and use your imagination. You can make a great film with imaginative editing and mediocre photography. But you can't make a great film with beautiful pictures and dull editing.

The important ideas of editing are:

1. The selection of the shots you want to use.
2. The order in which you put the shots together to make each scene. (You change the meaning of a scene when you rearrange the shots that make it up.)
3. The order in which the scenes are put together to build the sequences that make up the film.
4. The length of each shot and how that compares with the length of the shots around it. (Changes here change the whole impact of a scene.)

If your film has sync sound, of course you have to be concerned with what people are saying in each shot or scene. What they are saying has to make sense in the structure of the film.

EVEN WHEN YOU ARE WEARING EDITING GLOVES, HOLD FILM AT THE EDGE. THE EMULSION SCRATCHES EASILY

There are two methods of editing.

The first is to cut, edit, and project the developed, original reversal film. This method is the least expensive and most practical for experimental and beginning film work. But because the original material is being edited and projected, handle it *very* carefully to avoid dirt and scratching.

The second method is to have a work print made from the original film. Edit the work print, and then cut the original film to match the edited work print. If the original was a reversal, the edited original (or a print of it) can be projected. If the original was a negative, another print must be made for the projector.

The second method is preferred by filmmakers because the original material is handled the least and stays in good shape. This method also allows for printing corrections and optical work.

YOUR EDITING ROOM

You must have a space for editing that is clean and where you can leave your film out even when you are not working on it.

For editing you need:

1. A good sized hard-topped table.
2. A viewer through which you can hand-wind the film while you are looking at it. The viewer must have good illumination and a way to focus it so you can see each frame of your film clearly. There should be a smooth and simple way of threading the film into the viewer. It is handy to have a viewer that can notch the film at the frame you are seeing.

A VIEWER LETS YOU LOOK AT YOUR FILM IN MOTION, ONE FRAME AT A TIME. ALWAYS THREAD FILM IN THE VIEWER EMULSION SIDE UP

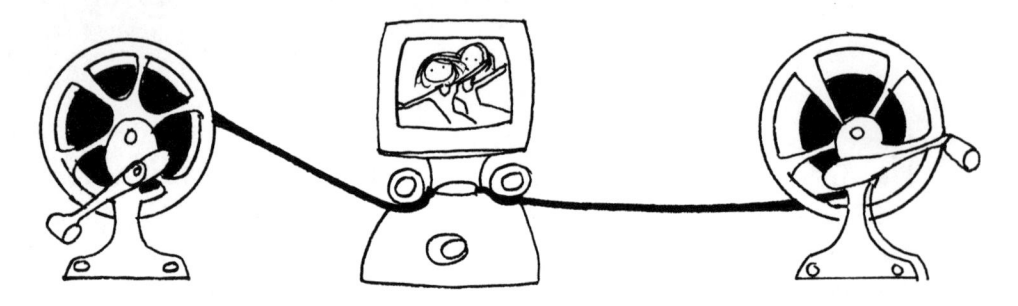

3. If the viewer does not have rewinds, you will need a pair of rewinds that can be attached to the table on each side of the viewer. The rewinds for Super 8 mm should be able to hold at least 400 foot reels.

4. At least a dozen reels, including one split reel and a flange.

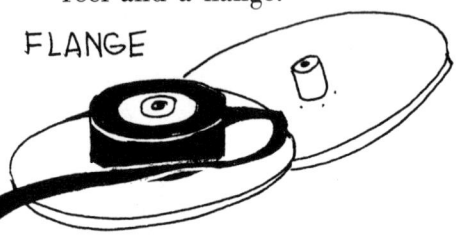

FLANGE

ONE KIND OF RACK FOR HOLDING REELS

5. A rack for holding reels. (You can make it or buy it.)

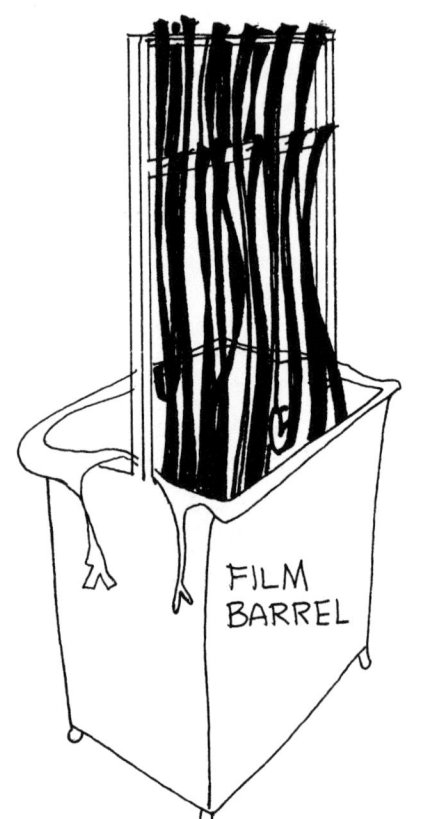

6. A splicer. There are two kinds, cement splicers and tape splicers. A cement splicer scrapes the film and the ends are joined by cementing. A tape splicer cuts and holds two pieces of film while you make a tape splice.

7. Editing cement or splicing tape.

8. Some kind of film barrel with a rack and pins for holding scenes while you are working. A professional barrel looks like this

FILM BARREL

But you can make your own. If you do, it's important to line it with cloth so the film won't get scratched or dirty.

9. A pair of scissors for cutting film.

10. Grease pencils and marker pen for marking.
11. One or two pairs of thin cotton editing gloves so your hands won't leave marks, dirt, or scratches. (These gloves are very cheap.)
12. A magnifying glass for looking at frames on the rack.
13. $\frac{1}{4}$-inch paper tape in dispenser.
14. Leader material, which is blank film for putting at the head and tail of sequences or between scenes.
15. A footage frame chart. (see page 92) Make a big copy of this to put over your editing table.
16. Single-edged razor blades.

If you are going to edit in sound, you need much more elaborate equipment. You need an editing machine that can run your separate sound tracks and film together at sound speed. There are several kinds. You also need a synchronizer, a sound reader, more time, and more money.

EDITING, STEP BY STEP

1. When your developed film or work print comes back from the laboratory, screen it. You must become very familiar with every foot of film you have. (Clean your projector first, so the film doesn't get scratched.) Make notes about the best scenes and those which are obviously unusable.

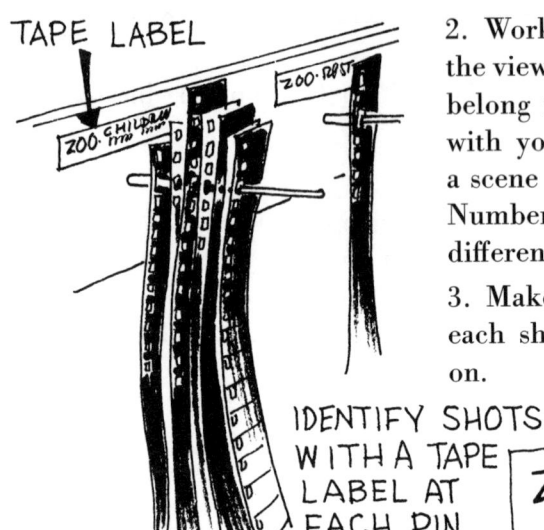

TAPE LABEL

2. Work on one scene at a time. First use the viewer to break down the shots you think belong in that scene. Cut the shots apart with your scissor and hang the "takes" of a scene together on a pin of your film rack. Number the pins. Hang different scenes on different pins.

3. Make a list giving a short description of each shot, and note what pin you hung it on.

IDENTIFY SHOTS WITH A TAPE LABEL AT EACH PIN

ZOO- CHILDREN FEEDING ANIMALS SCENE # 14

4. Study your list and work out an order for putting the shots together. There are many ways in which the same set of shots can be put together. When you are doing your filming, you have a particular idea in mind, and you shoot shots to show that idea. When you actually look at the shots, you may want to arrange them differently to express your original idea. You have much more freedom to do this in a silent film than one with dialog.

5. Now put the shots of a scene together in the order you have worked out from your shot list. Do this with paper tape or temporary splices, then look at them in the viewer.

TEMPORARY SPLICE MADE WITH PAPER TAPE (FOR SILENT EDITING)

76

Note: In order to get a feeling of the timing of the film, practice winding the film through the viewer at the same speed at which it will be projected.

6. Probably the scenes won't look right the first time. Now you will want to rearrange both the position and the length of the scenes. Whether you are looking at one sequence or at the whole film, keep asking yourself if you are accomplishing your objective as you cut the film.
Are you trying to communicate an emotion?
Report something factually?
Show clearly how something works?

7. When a sequence seems fairly well set, splice it together so you can screen it in a projector or editing machine. Make sure to splice the emulsion side of all the shots on the same side of your edited film. (If you are using tape splices, put a splice on both sides of the film before projecting it.) Projection is the only way to see if a sequence is really the way you want it.

8. Do this for each sequence, and then start joining sequences. You will find that as you start joining sequences you will want to make changes within a sequence or change their position to each other.

9. If some sequence really interrupts what you are trying to say, drop it, no matter how fond you are of the shots in it.

10. Keep making changes until you are really satisfied. If you find that you are missing a crucial scene, go out and shoot it if this is possible. It's worth the trouble.

ROLL, LABEL AND STACK SEQUENCES WITHIN EASY REACH

A FILM CAN IS A CLEAN AND HANDY PLACE TO KEEP SEQUENCES YOU ARE WORKING ON

77

```
  TAIL        FADE IN      HEAD
───────────────────────────────
───────────────╲─────────║─────
               ╲         ║
           FADE OUT
───────────────────────────────
─────────║────╱────────────────
         ║   ╱
            DISSOLVE
───────────────────────────────
             ╳╳
───────────────────────────────
```

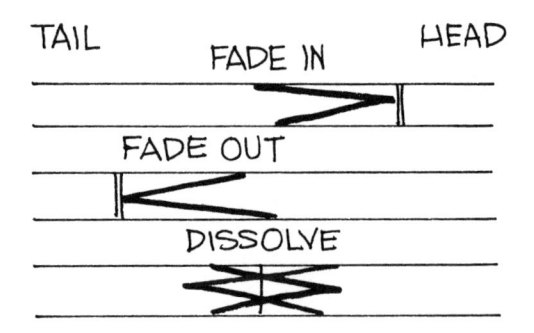

THESE SYMBOLS ARE GENERALLY USED FOR MARKING OPTICALS. USE A GREASE PENCIL

11. When you feel that your film is almost edited, if you are working with a work print, this is the time to figure out and mark all the places you want optical effects, such as fades and dissolves. If you are editing the original material, you are limited to the opticals you made in the camera while you were shooting.

12. If you are going to have titles, make them and edit them in now.

13. Your film is now ready for a first showing to an audience. Watch their reaction. If you don't seem to be getting your idea across the way you want to, try to figure out what new arrangement will communicate the idea better. Then do some re-editing, and try the film again on another audience.

14. Before doing a lot of projecting of your edited original, you might want to have a reversal copy made and save the original for special showings.

15. If you are going to add sound to your film, use the edited picture. Run it in the projector, and time out each sequence to decide what and how much sound you want. See pages 61–63 for ways of adding sound.

PROJECTORS

A projector is the final link in communicating a film idea to an audience. A lot of careful work can be lost if the projector does not do a good job, so do not underestimate its importance. If your funds are limited, it is better to buy a good, reconditioned, second-hand projector than a cheap, new one. A well-cared-for projector has a long life.

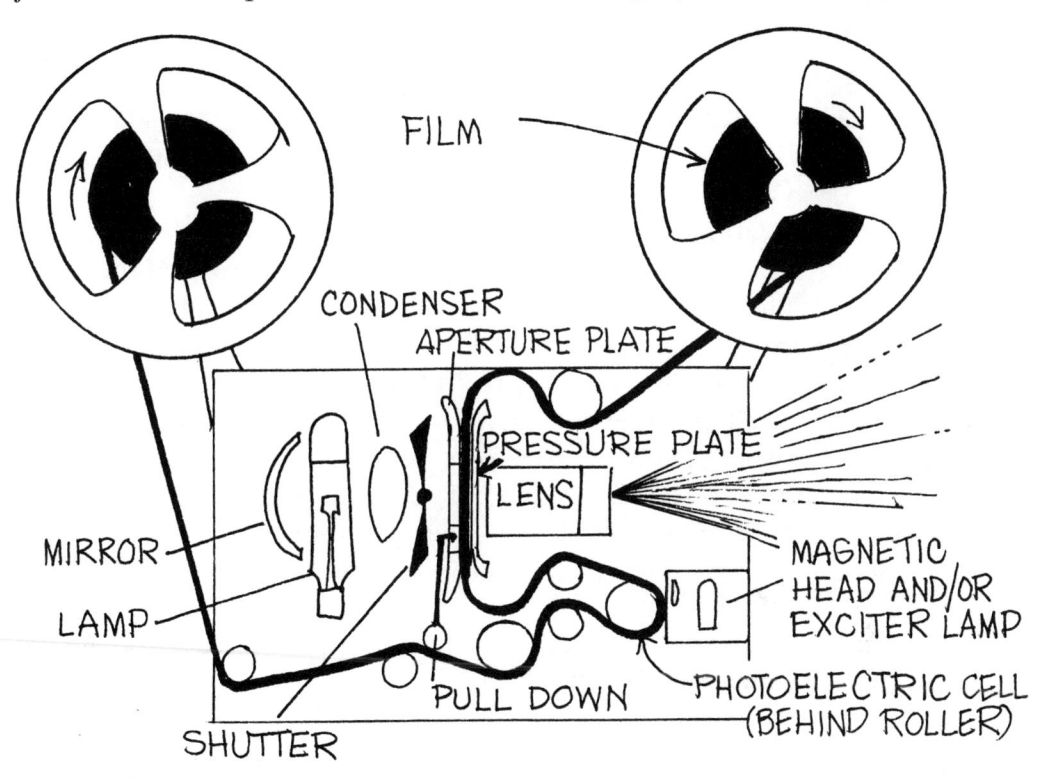

A projector has:
- a strong light with a system for focusing the light on the film;
- a shutter that interrupts the light when the film is moving;
- a mechanism for moving and stopping the film;
- a lens for focusing the picture on the screen;
- a means of controlling the speed of the moving film;
- reel arms for holding the film and a method for rewinding it; and
- an electric motor to run the whole thing.

In addition to these things, a sound projector has either an optical, or a magnetic, sound system, or both.

EDISON'S *KINETOSCOPE* WAS THE FIRST WAY OF LOOKING AT FILMS

You have to thread some projectors. If yours is like this, thread it carefully. If the film is not threaded properly, it can be torn, scratched, or burned. (This is the danger of using original material.) If film isn't threaded properly, the picture can be jumpy or out of frame. Incorrect threading can put a sound film out of sync.

Some projectors are self-threading. You just feed the leader into a guide and turn on the projector. One problem with a self-threading projector is that it is difficult to remove the film in the middle of a reel. While you are working with your film, often you will want to run just part of a sequence, then take the reel off to make a change.

Another kind of projector allows you to load a reel of film into a cartridge. Then, when the cartridge is put into the projector, the film is automatically threaded. This kind of projector also allows you to rewind the film, rapidly, back onto the reel, at any point in the film.

Some projectors only use cartridges in which the finished film has been loaded and sealed.

Self-threading and cartridge projectors are better for people who are only viewing films, not making them.

Some projector lenses are "faster" than others. The speed of a projector lens is shown by an f number. An f 1.6 is a faster lens than an f 3.5. The faster the lens, the more light comes through it to the screen from the same bulb.

Projector lenses are also marked in focal lengths. The shorter the focal length, the bigger the picture at a particular distance.

THE *MAGIC LANTERN* WAS ONE OF THE EARLIEST PROJECTORS. IT PROJECTED SLIDES

SHORT FOCAL LENGTH   LONGER   LONGEST

THE SHORTER THE FOCAL LENGTH OF THE LENS, THE SHORTER THE THROW TO THE SCREEN FOR THE SAME SIZE IMAGE

Before you buy a projector and lens, try to figure out the projection distance you will be using and how big a picture you want. The bigger the picture, or the longer the throw, the faster the lens should be. Very short, very long, or very fast lenses are expensive.

Zoomar projector lenses allow you to change the size of your picture at a given distance. These are convenient. Check to see if they fit your requirements and your budget.

Projectors (either Super 8 mm or 16 mm) with magnetic sound systems can be used to record the sound directly onto an edited film that has a magnetic stripe. (See p. 60, 63)

GOOD PROJECTING HABITS

Make sure you fill out and mail the warranty on a new projector. On a used projector, get a written guarantee from the dealer.

Read carefully the directions for using and taking care of your projector and follow them. Even if you buy a projector second hand, be sure to get the instruction book.

Keep the projector clean. Clean the projecting lens with a lens tissue. Clean the condensing lenses with tissue too.

Clean the gate and aperture plate regularly. If emulsion has collected anywhere, use your thumbnail or a wooden stick to scrape it off. Never use anything metal. It will scratch the parts, and they will scratch your film. Brush out or blow out dust and emulsion with a brush or air bulb. Do this from the side, with the gate open, and from the front, by removing the lens.

Oil the projector only according to the instructions. If you use too much oil it will get on your film.

Have your projector serviced by an authorized dealer regularly. Make sure that he checks the pressure on the pressure plate.

Always have a spare bulb for your projector. If it's an optical sound projector, have a spare exciter lamp. Most 8 mm projectors have 150 watt lights. Most 16 mm projectors have 750 or 1000 watt bulbs. Be sure to get the proper wattage and base.

The instant you see your film begin to jump or slip, shut the projector off. Do not try to re-establish the loop with your finger while the projector is running. In fact, the instant *anything* looks, sounds, or smells funny, stop the projector.

When you have finished your screening, continue to run the projector with the bulb off so the fan can cool everything evenly.

When you are not using your projector, keep it covered.

In screening sound film, experiment until you find the right placement for your speaker, a good sound level for the size of your room, and a proper tone quality.

IN 1910, EUGENE LAUSTE, WORKING AT THE EDISON LABORATORY, MADE THE FIRST OPTICAL SOUND TRACK

PROJECTION SCREENS

Walls are to hold a building up; poster board is to draw on; a motion picture screen is to see motion pictures on.

A proper screen makes an enormous difference in the way an audience sees your film. If the surface isn't right, your picture will lose brightness. If the surface isn't true white, the color will be off.

There are two basic kinds of screens. A glass beaded screen gives sharper, brighter pictures. But a matte screen has a wider angle of viewing. They are about the same price.

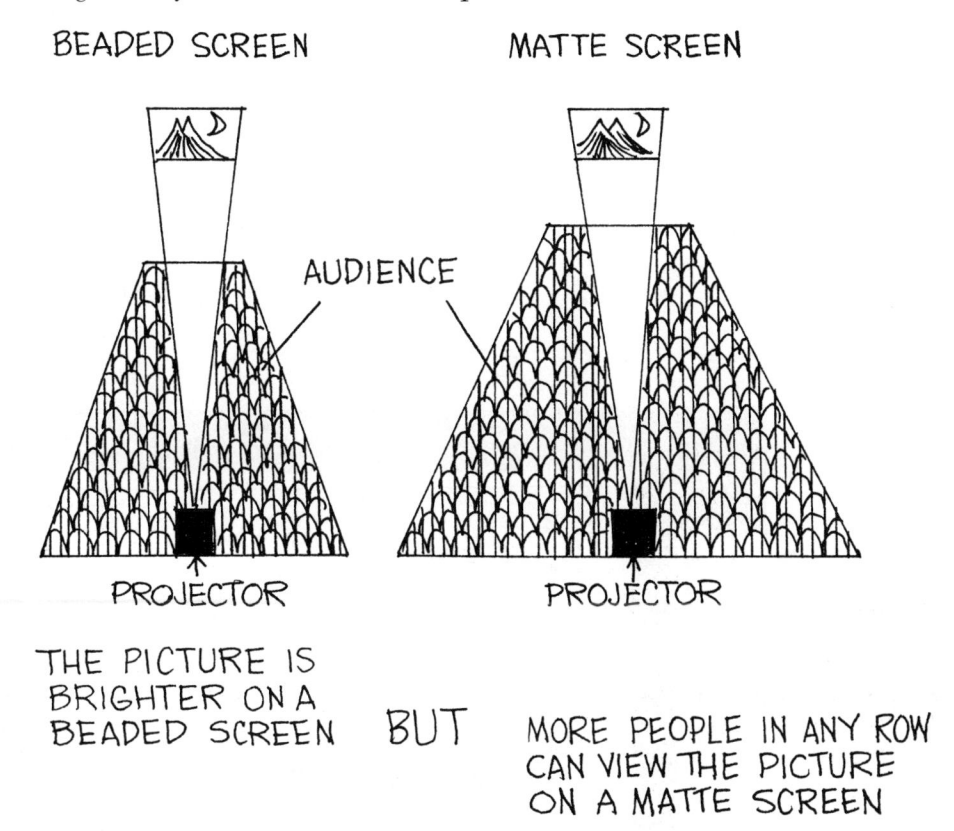

BEADED SCREEN / MATTE SCREEN

AUDIENCE

PROJECTOR / PROJECTOR

THE PICTURE IS BRIGHTER ON A BEADED SCREEN   BUT   MORE PEOPLE IN ANY ROW CAN VIEW THE PICTURE ON A MATTE SCREEN

When you are setting up your film showing, try to arrange the seats so that everyone has a clear view of the screen without having to lean around the person in front. Attention to all the details of screening your film will pay off in audience enjoyment, even if you have an audience of only one—yourself.

WHERE YOUR FILM CAN BE SHOWN

Probably there are a lot of people who would like to see your film. So you, as the producer, should set up a series of showings.

First, to all the people who helped make the film—actors, crew, sponsors, advisors.

If your film group is in a school or a neighborhood center, show it there.

If the film is of community interest, arrange to show it at community meetings.

Exchange it for films made by other film groups. They will be interested in seeing what you are doing.

You can even set up a film festival with other filmmakers and charge admission.

If you feel that your film is really good, submit it as an entry in an established film festival.

FILMING WORDS

ANSWER PRINT. The first print from the original, edited film in which all differences in brightness and color from shot to shot have been corrected.

APERTURE PLATE. A metal plate with a frame-sized opening against which film is pressed as it goes through the camera or projector.

ASA NUMBER. A number in a standard system that shows the speed of a film.

AUXILIARY FINDER. A finder for looking at the picture through a lens that matches, but is separate from, the camera lens.

BRIDGE. A connection between two scenes.

CARTRIDGE. A container in which unexposed film is packaged for feeding through the camera, or finished film is packaged for feeding through a projector.

CASSETTE. A cartridge, usually containing magnetic tape.

CHANGING BAG. A light-tight cloth bag in which you can put your arms to load or unload undeveloped film, into, or out of, a magazine in daylight.

CINEMATOGRAPHER. A head cameraman.

CINEMA VERITE. A technique of filming that combines a fictional story with real situations and films them in a largely unrehearsed, spontaneous way.

CLOSE-UP. A close shot.

COMPOSITION. The arrangement of the elements in the picture.

CORE. A small, plastic hub around which film is wound.

CONTINUITY. The progression of scenes that make up a film.

CRAWL. A moving strip with credits printed on it.

CREDITS. The names on the screen of people who helped make the film.

CUT. A piece of film that has been trimmed to a desired length.
To CUT film is to edit or arrange it in sequences of a desired order.
To CUT a scene is to shorten it or take it out.
"CUT!" A command to stop the cameras or the action.
CU. abbreviation for close-up.
DAILIES. A print of each day's filming, developed and screened as quickly as possible after shooting.
DIRECTION OF ACTION. Which way an action moves on the screen.
DISSOLVE. An overlapping fade-out, fade-in, used as a bridge between two scenes.
DOLLY. A platform on wheels for a camera mount.
EDGE NUMBERS. Reference numbers, printed on the edge of raw stock. They are counting numbers so any point on the film can be identified. They are important in cutting a negative to match a work print.
EMULSION. The photosensitive chemical coating on film.
EMULSION NUMBER. The identifying number assigned by the manufacturer to each batch of film it makes.
EXCITER LAMP. A light in a camera or a projector that changes its brightness in recording or playing sound.
EXPOSURE METER. An instrument for measuring the amount of light that falls on, or is reflected from, an object. It has a scale so you can figure out your film exposure.
FADE (-in or -out). An effect that makes the picture gradually appear or disappear at the beginning or end of a scene.
FINDER (VIEW FINDER). A camera attachment for seeing a view of the picture that will be taken.
FIXED FOCUS LENS. A lens whose focal length does not change.
FLANGE. A one-sided, solid reel on which film is wound on a core. It can then be removed and kept without the reel.
f NUMBER. The number that indicates the fastest speed of a lens.

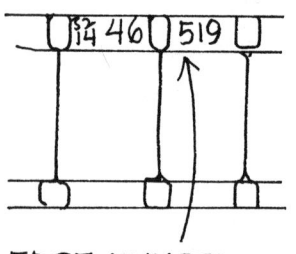

EDGE NUMBERS (IN 16mm FILM THERE IS A NEW CONSECUTIVE NUMBER EVERY 20 FRAMES)

FOCAL LENGTH. The distance between the optical center of a lens and the plane at which an object at infinity focuses. The shorter the focal length, the wider the angle, and the smaller things are in the picture. The longer the focal length, the narrower the angle, and the larger things are in the picture.

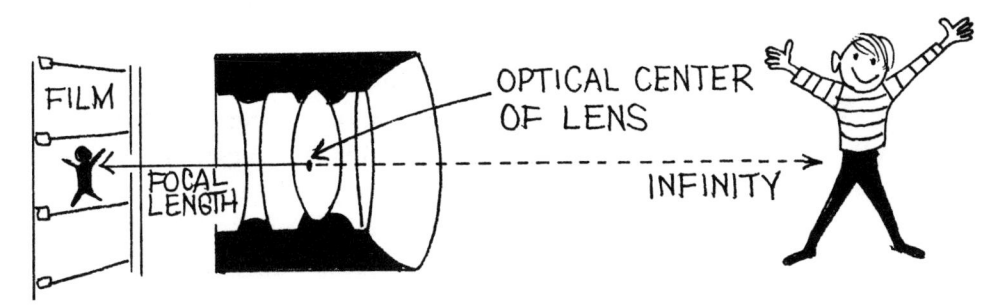

FOCUSING MOUNT. The mechanism for moving a lens in and out to focus it.
FRAME. A single picture. To frame means to include in the picture.
f STOP. A number that tells you how far the lens is open or closed down.
GATE. The group of parts in a camera or projector consisting of the aperture plate, the pressure plate, and the pull-down, through which the film passes behind the lens.
HEAD. The beginning of a shot, a sequence, or a reel of film.
INSERT. A shot, usually a close-up, that is put into a scene to show the details of something.
IN SYNC. Where the picture and the sound are matched.
IRIS. A mechanism for controlling the amount of light that comes through a lens.
"IT'S IN THE CAN." An expression of satisfaction when a scene has been successfully filmed.
LEADER. Special film stock, either black or white, which is spliced to the head and tail of film during editing. It is also used to mark a place where a missing shot or scene will be inserted. An academy leader is a leader of standard length used in all sound synchronization and projection.

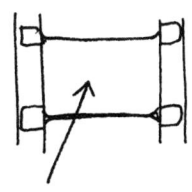

LENS. A combination of shaped glass elements that can focus an image onto a surface.

MAGAZINE. A container for holding unexposed film. It can be in the camera or attached to the outside. (See also *cartridge*.)

MAGNETIC SOUND. A method of sound recording that changes sound into magnetic variations on a tape.

MCU. Medium close-up.

MOUNTING. Putting developed film on reels.

MOVIEOLA. One kind of sound editing machine.

MIX. The process of combining and balancing various sound tracks into a single track.

MIXER. An electronic device for combining the feeds from more than one sound source (microphone, record player, tape machine) into one output feed with matched levels.

NEGATIVE FILM. The kind of film which, when developed, produces a negative image.

ONE SHOT. A shot of one person, singled out from a group.

OPTICAL EFFECTS. Fades, dissolves, superimpositions, and other special effects, produced either in the camera or by special printing methods.

OPTICAL SOUND. Sound which is recorded and printed as a photographic image on the film.

OUT OF FRAME. In filming, something which is out of, or goes out of the picture. In the projector, when the picture frame on the film does not line up with the aperture in the projector.

PANNING. Pivoting the camera to create the same effect as scanning a scene by turning your head.

PRESSURE PLATE. The plate that holds film flat while each frame is exposed in the camera or projected in the projector.

PRINTING. Making a copy from either a negative or reversal film.

PROCESSING. Developing film.

RAW STOCK. Unexposed film.

REFLEX FINDER. A way of looking at the picture through the taking lens, even when the camera is running.
REVERSAL FILM. Film which, when developed, results in a positive image.
RIGHTS. The ownership, or license to use, material.
ROUGH CUT. Assembling the shots in a sequence in some logical order without concern for length.
RUSHES. Same as DAILIES.
SCALE. Established union wages for any job.
SCENE. A single event. It may be one shot, but usually is a group of shots.
SEQUENCE. A group of related scenes.
SHOOTING. Filming.
SHOOTING SCRIPT. A breakdown of the script into individual shots in the order in which they will be filmed.
SHOOTING SCHEDULE. The order in which various elements of the production are planned.
SHOT. A single take, from the time the camera starts running until it stops.
SHOT LIST. The list of shots in a film.
SHUTTER. The device that opens and closes to allow light through to the film for an exposure.
SHUTTER SPEED. The fraction of a second that the shutter is open for making an exposure.
SILENT SPEED. The speed of silent film, which is 16 or 18 frames per second. This gives the same amount of screen time as sound speed but uses one-third less film.
SLATE. A device for identifying any part of a film and establishing a sync mark on both the film and the track.
SOUND SPEED. 24 frames per second, which is needed to record good quality optical sound.
SOUND TRACK. The sound component of a film. It can be recorded as an optical or magnetic track.
SPLICE. To join two pieces of film together.

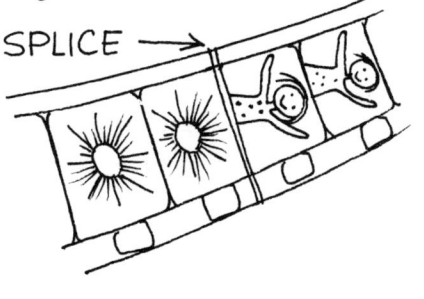

SYNCHRONOUS (SYNC) SOUND. Sound that precisely matches the action on the film. The sound and picture are electronically linked and recorded together.
TACHOMETER. A device that shows how fast the film is moving through the camera.
TAIL. The end of a shot, a sequence, or a reel.
TAKE. One of several shots of the same action.
THREAD. To lace film through the mechanism of a camera or projector.
THROW. The distance between the projector and the screen.
TRACK. The recorded sound.
TILTING. Panning the camera up or down.
TUNGSTEN. Artificial light.
TWO SHOT. A shot of two people out of a group.
VIEW FINDER. See *finder*.

WIDE-ANGLE SHOT. Any shot that takes in more picture than the normal angle for a particular film size. (See table on p. 91)
WILD SOUND. Sound not recorded in synchronization with the film.
WORK PRINT. A copy made from original negative or reversal film, to be used in editing. A one-light work print is an uncorrected work print, made with an average setting on the printing machine.
ZOOMAR. A lens with a variable focal length.

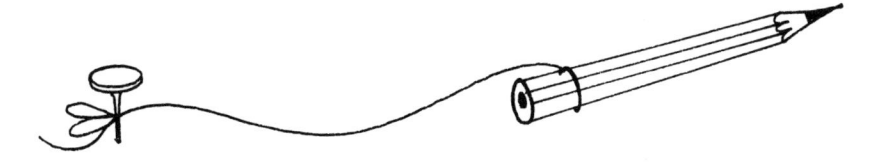

SOME HANDY CHARTS

WHICH LENS FOR WHICH PICTURE?

Film Size	Wide-Angle Picture Lens Size	Normal Picture Lens Size	Medium Telephoto Picture Lens Size	Long Telephoto Picture Lens Size
8 mm	8 mm	12 mm	25 mm	40 mm
Super 8 mm	9 mm	14 mm	40 mm	60 mm
16 mm	9.5–15 mm	25 mm	100 mm	200 mm
35 mm	28 mm	50 mm	150 mm	300 mm

CAMERA SHUTTER SPEED TABLE

Camera Speed
(frames per second)

Shutter Speed
(fractions of a second approx.)

8	1/15	
16	1/30	
18	1/33	(normal Super 8 mm speed)
24	1/45	(normal professional sound speed)
32	1/60	
48	1/90	
64	1/120	

RUNNING TIMES AND FILM LENGTHS FOR COMMON PROJECTION SPEEDS

Film Format	8mm (80 Frames per Foot)	Super 8 (72 Frames per Foot)		16 mm (40 Frames per Foot)	
Projection Speed in Frames per Second	18	18	24	18	24
Running Time and Film Length	Feet + Frames	Feet + Frames	Feet + Frames	Feet + Frames	Feet + Frames
Seconds 1	0 18	0 18	0 24	0 18	0 24
2	0 36	0 36	0 48	0 36	1 8
3	0 54	0 54	1 0	1 14	1 32
4	0 72	1 0	1 24	1 32	2 16
5	1 10	1 18	1 48	2 10	3 0
6	1 28	1 36	2 0	2 28	3 24
7	1 46	1 54	2 24	3 6	4 8
8	1 64	2 0	2 48	3 24	4 32
9	2 2	2 18	3 0	4 2	5 16
10	2 20	2 36	3 24	4 20	6 0
Minutes 1	13 40	15 0	20 0	27 0	36 0
2	27 0	30 0	40 0	54 0	72 0
3	40 40	45 0	60 0	81 0	108 0
4	54 0	60 0	80 0	108 0	144 0
5	67 40	75 0	100 0	135 0	180 0

EQUIPMENT SOURCES

Here are some of the places where you can buy or rent equipment. They all have catalogues which you can write for. Also look in the yellow pages of the telephone book under MOTION PICTURES for the companies and laboratories in your area.

Behrends Inc.
161 East Grand Street
Chicago, Illinois 60611

Birns & Sawyer
1026 N. Highland Avenue
Los Angeles, California 90038

Camera Sales Center Corp.
333 West 52 Street
New York, New York 10019

F & B / Ceco Inc.
315 West 43 Street,
New York, New York 10036

Ceco also has branches in Hollywood, California; Hialeah, Florida; Washington D.C.; Atlanta, Georgia; Cleveland, Ohio.

Cine' Tech Inc.
801 NW 111 Street
Miami, Florida 33168

Cinevision
200 Northcliffe Avenue
Montreal, Quebec, Canada

Victoria Duncan Inc.
2659 Fondren
Dallas, Texas 75206
   (also in Detroit and Chicago)

The *Motion Picture TV & Theater Directory*, Tarrytown, New York 10591 has a good listing of many services, laboratories, music libraries, and rental facilities that are useful to filmmakers. Many of these are in the New York area. The directory is published twice a year.

PERIODICALS

The following periodicals give news and information of interest to young filmmakers about film festivals, new films available, competitions, reviews, interviews, equipment, and techniques.

American Cinematographer
P.O. Box 2230
Hollywood, California 90028

Canyon Cinema News
263 Colgate
Berkeley, California 94708

Cinema Canada
Canadian Society of Cinematologists
2533 Gerrard Street East
Scarborough, Ontario, Canada

Cineaste
27 West 11 Street
New York, New York 10011

Filmmakers Newsletter
80 Wooster Street
New York, New York 10012

Making Films in New York
49 West 45 Street
New York, New York 10036

Take One
Box 1778, Station B
Montreal 110, Quebec, Canada

REFERENCE BOOKS

Handbook of Basic Motion Picture Techniques
Brodbeck, Emil E.
Published by: Chilton Books

How to Make Good Movies
Eastman Kodak
(Eastman Kodak has many excellent booklets on individual subjects.)

American Cinematographer's Manual
Published by: American Society of Cinematographers, Hollywood

The Technique of Editing 16 mm Films
Burder, John
Publisher: Hastings House

Young Filmmakers
Rodger Larson with Ellen Meade
Publisher: E. P. Dutton & Co.

Elements of Film
Bobker, Lee R.R.
Publisher: Harcourt, Brace and World

The Technique of Film Animation
John Halas and Roger Manvell
Published by: Focus Press

INDEX

animation, 24, 67–69
art director, 10
audience, 12, 84

cameraman (cinematographer), 8, 9
cameras, 42–51, 91
   lenses, 48–51, 91
   sixteen millimeter, 45–47
   super 8 millimeter, 43–44
continuity girl, 9

director, 8, 9
documentaries, 13–15, 35
dramatic stories, 15–17

editing, *see* films
expenses, 18–24

film, 41, 54–56
filming, 30–39
   accessories, 52–53
   slow motion, 65
   speeded-up action, 64
   time-lapse photography, 64
film makers, organizations, 7
films:
   dramatic stories, 15–17
   documentaries, 13–15, 35
   editing of, 8, 11, 15, 23, 27, 38, 72–78

   explanation of, 40
   reporting events, 12
   types of, 5
   viewpoint, 12
financing, 25

gaffer, 10
grips, 10

lighting, 10, 31, 57–59

musical director, 10

persistence of vision, 40
producer, 8
production manager, 9
production schedules, 26–29
projectors and projecting, 79–83, 92
props, 11

releases, 33
reporting events, 12

scripts, 12, 16, 17
set designer, 10
sound, 10, 60–63

titles and credits, 23, 66

writer, 8